THE COSMATI

TOMB OF HENRY III. NORTH FACE
WESTMINSTER ABBEY

Petrus Odarisi

THE COSMATI

THE ROMAN MARBLE WORKERS OF THE XIIth AND XIIIth CENTURIES

by

EDWARD HUTTON

. . . the bright
Pavement that like a Sea of Jasper shon
Impurpl'd with Celestial Roses smil'd.

Paradise Lost, iii, 362-4

LONDON
ROUTLEDGE AND KEGAN PAUL LTD

Published in England
by ROUTLEDGE & KEGAN PAUL LTD.
Broadway House, 68-74 Carter Lane
London E.C.4
1950

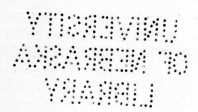
Printed in Great Britain at The Westminster Press
411a Harrow Road, London W.9

To

GEORGE AND JANET TREVELYAN

MUSIS AMICIS

I have especially to thank my old friend the Rt. Rev. Dom Philip Langdon, O.S.B., Titular Abbot of Abingdon, who has taken endless trouble both now and formerly to obtain for me photographs of the works, and especially of the pavements of the "Cosmati". Indeed, but for his intervention in 1939-40, I should never have received from Italy the material necessary for the pavements in St. Paul's Chapel in Westminster Cathedral and in Buckfast Abbey Church; and now I am in his debt again for the photographs of the pavement in the Badia di Farfa and the ciborium of S. Andrea in Flumine near Ponzano Romano.

CONTENTS

LIST OF PLATES
(end of book)

ix

THE ROMAN MARBLE
CRAFTSMEN
AND
THEIR WORKS

THE ROMAN MARBLE CRAFTSMEN
AND THEIR WORKS

I

A DREAM between sleeping and waking, anticipating the Renaissance of the XVth century is what we discern in the Roman art of the XIIth and XIIIth centuries. Rome, aware if only for a moment of her past, opposes her Classical spirit and tradition to the half barbarian Lombard and Gothic styles. And here in Rome itself we have the highest achievement of the Roman school in the cloister of S. Giovanni in Laterano, the work of the Vassalletti. Order, constructional regularity, harmony, balance, beauty of design and colour — these are the marks of the Roman art of the XIIth and XIIIth centuries as they were of the Classical age and the art of the Renaissance.

It is delightful to spend a leisurely winter in Rome—if indeed modern Rome allows of leisure, that leisure which fifty years ago was a part of her dignity—in renewing an old enjoyment of the noble works of the *marmorari romani*.

It is even more delightful to while away a spring and summer in the country, seeking out once more these beautiful things in the little fierce cities of Latium, on the fringes of Etruria and Abruzzo, in the hill towns of Umbria and even in Tuscany. They lie north, south and east of Rome, the little ancient cities where in Cathedral or parish church these works of the *marmorari romani* most abound; in Anagni where there is a group of the best of them in the Cathedral in which Alexander III canonised S. Edward Confessor, received the submission of Henry II after the murder of Becket, excommunicated Frederick II, *Stupor Mundi*, and where Boniface VIII was outraged, assaulted and driven mad by the emissaries of Philip le Bel; in Ferentino too, in Cori, in Terracina and in Fondi. All these are south of Rome, above the Sacco valley on the Hernician foothills, or aloft over the Pontine marshes where Ninfa used to hold the last enchantments of the Middle age, or beyond the Circean mount on the confines of Campania.

North of Rome there is Città Castellana where, in the Duomo façade, portico and triumphal arch, we have achievements which rival the Lateran cloister in beauty and harmony, the work of three generations of the Cosmati, father, son and grandson. In Viterbo too, the church of S. Francesco holds three tombs of the school —a pavement and a rose window. West of Viterbo we shall find the great church of S. Maria in Castello at Tarquinia and the abandoned church of S. Pietro at Tuscania (Toscanella) with their magnificent Roman façades and portals, for the most part the work of the Ranucii family.

But what we seek we shall find again outside the little cities in the now abandoned or half abandoned abbey churches and basilicas with their long and lovely names: S. Andrea in Flumine, S. Maria di Falleri, Castel S. Elia, Badia di S. Antimo a Nazzano,

S. Giovanni in Argentella, S. Maria in Vescovio, S. Maria in Vulturella, Badia di Farfa, places almost unknown save to the archæologist and the lover of the *marmorari romani;* places always of great beauty, half lost in a countryside as strange and as beautiful as themselves.

What for instance could be lovelier, what more strange and unexpected than the Badia di Castel S. Elia, its wonderful basilica hidden in a volcanic gorge watered by a murmuring stream and filled with trees and groves, to be reached down more than a hundred steps and long abandoned; tended now by Franciscan friars. There on the beautiful mosaic pavement, before an apse covered with frescoes of the Roman school you may see the simplest and yet perhaps for that reason the most beautiful of the ciboria for which the Roman school is famous, and, still in a dream, climb the hundred steps and leave so strange, so beautiful, so silent a place.

What could be more strange indeed, unless it be S. Andrea in Flumine near Ponzano Romano at the end of a steep and difficult byway under the wooded hills by the Tiber, it too with its Cosmati pavement, its signed ciborium, its screen and altar and its ambone of 1209. Or there is the Badia di S. Antimo above Nazzano with its rude portico, its three aisles divided by six columns, its apse with frescoes of the XVth century, its much ruined but still beautiful pavement, its schola cantorum and ambone and its wonderful view.

What again could be more strange than S. Maria di Falleri, near Città Castellana, abandoned, like S. Maria in Vescovio on the other side of the Tiber, in the ruins of a famous Roman city and fortress, the Roman walls and fortifications all round the ruined and abandoned church, which still retains its noble portal signed by Laurentius and his son Jacobus. Not far off is Nepi where hardly anything belonging to the Cosmati is left us; but Sutri, further on, still retains though restored, its superb mosaic pavement. All these places are within the influence, if not the shadow, of Monte Soracte, about to break like a wave over the wide Tiber valley and the Campagna of Rome.

On the other side of the Tiber in the Sabina we find the very ancient and lonely abbey of Farfa, once the richest and most powerful in Italy and now fallen to nothing, its only treasure perhaps the rich and lovely mosaic pavement, pieced together it is true, but glorious still in its decadence. There we find the name Rainaldus who worked here no doubt on other things.

And then quite as surprising and beautiful in its own fashion, difficult too to approach, is S. Giovanni in Argentella near Palombara Sabina, a basilica of the XIIth century with apses and Roman campanile, and within, an iconostasis with its small columns and architrave, the only one I know, save the reconstruction in S. Maria in Cosmedin, inscribed and dated 1170 together with an earlier ciborium.[1]

Then there is, also in the Aniene, the valley of the Anio, S. Maria in Vulturella (commonly called Mentorella) amid fantastic rocks with its fragment of pavement,

[1] Palombara Sabina, Vulturella in the Aniene and Farfa in Sabina are best reached from Rome especially since the bridge under Poggio Mirteto has been destroyed and not yet (1949) rebuilt.

its twisted column, the remains of a candelabrum, and its fine ciborium, not to mention its bronze processional cross and fragment of bronze reliquary, finely sculptured and other treasures of the XIIth century.

I have named the Latian confines of Etruria and Abruzzo where in and about Orvieto, at Lugnano in Teverina for instance, there is a fine portico, façade and crypt; and in Orvieto itself a pulpit in S. Andrea and Arnolfo's magnificent tomb of Cardinal de Braye in S. Domenico; at Alba Fucense and at Rocca di Botte in Abruzzo, there is in the former, in spite of the earthquake of 1915 which destroyed nearly everything, an ambone, or the remains of it, and at the latter both ambone and ciborium.

Indeed one might well, as the summer deepens, find one's way into the Umbrian hills where at Narni over the Nera valley with its charming inn, as friendly as the Albergo Flaminio at Città Castellana, there are fragments of Cosmati pavements in the Cathedral and in S. Domenico and a shrine of the school in S. Maria in Pensola.

Further north S. Francesco in Assisi is rich in Cosmati work and at Bevagna one finds a magnificent costmatesque portal in S. Michele, signed by Binellus and Ridolfus and a similar portal probably by the same masters, perhaps local craftsmen, in the porta minore of the Duomo of Foligno, while at Sassovivo near by there is the fine cloister signed by masters of the Roman school.

Even into Tuscany, as we may see in Florence, Pisa and Lucca, the influence of the Roman school penetrated not least of course by means of the Tuscan master Arnolfo di Cambio.

And so it is that though the Roman school, already ceasing to be Roman, was to perish altogether with the departure of the Papacy to Avignon, it finds an echo in the art of Giotto and thus in the main development of Italian art; but its final justification, if indeed it needs any justification save its own beauty, comes with the Renaissance of the XVth century and the return to antiquity, out of which has arisen most of what we hold dear in the art, culture and civilization of what till yesterday was the civilized world.

II

THE Renaissance of art in Rome in the XIIth century, though a false dawn, was a true Renaissance inspired as it was by a direct study of the antique as well as of the Byzantine art of Sicily and Campania. Rome recalling her past greatness after unspeakable disaster began to adorn herself under Popes Paschal II (1094-1118), Honorius II (1124-1130), Innocent II (1120-1140) and again under Popes Innocent III (1198-1216) and Honorius III (1216-1227) and throughout the XIIIth century. This like the Renaissance of the XVth century was essentially a lay movement by a well-defined school of craftsmen. Guilds and workshops appear. Roman artists and craftsmen had always been organized according to their occupations, and even confined to a certain region, quarter or street with a *schola*, where the craft descended from father to son. And it is indeed families of craftsmen one finds in Rome about 1100 A.D. These families have in modern times become famous as the 'Cosmati', though such a family name had no existence; this name however has been used to include more or less all the families of craftsmen of the *marmorari romani;* and the work done in marble or mosaic in pavements, altars, ciboria, ambones, Paschal candlesticks, Bishops' thrones, tombs, and so forth, is known as "Cosmati work", *arte Cosmatesca.* Masters of decoration, these men handed their traditions from father to son generation after generation. We can name four or five of these families as well as a number of independent craftsmen.

The earliest was the family of Paulus, who in the time of Paschal II worked in Rome and at Ferentino, and his sons who made the ciborium of S. Lorenzo fuori le mura, while his grandson worked at Sutri, Gaeta and in Rome.

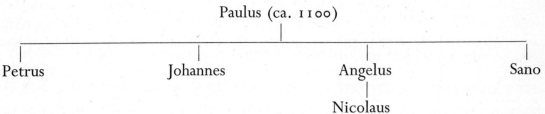

Paulus (ca. 1100)

Petrus   Johannes   Angelus   Sano

Nicolaus

Another family was that of Rainerius or Ranucius and his sons and grandsons whose work is to be found at Tarquinia and elsewhere.

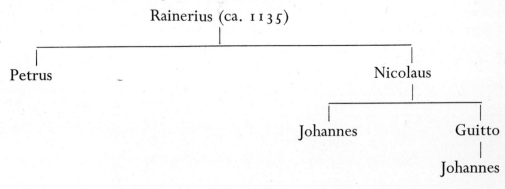

Rainerius (ca. 1135)

Petrus   Nicolaus

Johannes   Guitto

Johannes

In the XIIIth century there is the family of Drudus de Trivio who made the ciborium at Anagni and who appears at Lanuvio with his son Angelo.

But of all these dynasties the most celebrated are those of Laurentius and Vassallettus. Of the former the head is Laurentius son of Thebaldus (op. 1162-1200) who had for son Jacobus (op. 1185-1217) and for grandson Cosmas (op. 1210-1231), of whom was born Lucas (op. 1231-1235) and Jacobus (op. 1231-1235).

Their work is to be seen at Città Castellana and at Subiaco and Anagni and in Rome at S. Maria in Aracoeli, at S. Saba and S. Tommaso in Formis and elsewhere.

The family of Vassallettus (ca. 1150) and his son Petrus and grandson Vassallettus III was especially practised in sculpture. Their work is to be seen in the Paschal candlestick in S. Paolo fuori le mura, in the cloister there and at S. Giovanni in Laterano and in the Episcopal throne and Paschal candlestick at Anagni.

Lastly, though Venturi refuses to consider this a separate family from the Laurentian, and he may be right, we have Cosmas II or Cosmatus (op. 1276) and his sons Jacobus, Petrus, Iohannes and Deodatus. Their work is to be found in the Sancta Sanctorum chapel, in the ciborio of S. Maria in Cosmedin by Deodatus and in various works in Rome, in Viterbo and perhaps in Westminster Abbey.

There was also a number of other craftsmen *marmorari*, not grouped in families: Paschalis who made the Paschal candlestick in S. Maria in Cosmedin: Rusticus who worked at S. Giovanni in Argentella near Palombara; Andreas, Iohannes and Petrus who made the ambone in S. Pietro at Alba Fucense; Petrus de Maria the builder of the cloister at Sassovivo near Foligno. There were also the Rainaldus who made the pavement in the Badia of Farfa in Sabina, the Ivo who worked at Vicovaro, and others.

The centre of the activity of the "Cosmati" was Rome and they seem to have been established among the ruins of the ancient City where they found not only their most precious materials, porphyry columns and verde antico which they cut up into discs and rounds and four square pieces of various size and into small *tesserae*, but the forms and sometimes the very objects, sculptured capitals, architraves, and again lions and sphinxes, which they studied as models or copied with devoted integrity and a sound taste that almost amounted to inspiration. The lions and sphinx in the screens at Città Castellana, or the Sphinxes in the Lateran cloister or that of Frate Pasquale at Viterbo bear witness to this.

The chief influence after antiquity itself in the development of this school of *marmorari romani* was that of the contemporary Siculo-Campanian school of Byzantine art in South Italy and Palermo, the points of contact being Terracina, Gaeta, Montecassino, Capua, Amalfi and Salerno.

The perfection of this Roman art is found between the XIIth century and the third quarter of the XIIIth century and its most glorious architectural achievements in Rome are the campanili of S. Maria in Cosmedin and other churches (Plates 1-3); the cloisters of S. Giovanni in Laterano (Plates 6-8) and S. Paolo fuori le mura (Plates 5a, 9b), the porticoes of S. Lorenzo fuori le mura (Plate 14) and of S. Giorgio in Velabro (Plate 3), the portal of S. Tommaso in Formis (Plate 15b), and outside

Rome the cloisters of S. Scholastica at Subiaco (Plate 9a) and of the Badia of Sassovivo (Plate 10a) and above all the portico of the Duomo of Città Castellana (Plates 16-18) where in 1210 Jacobus with Cosmas *filio suo carissimo* signed the magnificent triumphal arch.

Later there enters a gothic influence into the school perhaps from the Cistercian Abbeys such as Fossanova, perhaps from Tuscany, for Arnolfo di Cambio had, it might seem, been an associate of the Roman school, as would appear in his glorious tomb of Cardinal de Braye in S. Domenico at Orvieto. His ciboria in S. Paolo fuori lem ra (1265) and in S. Cecilia in Trastevere (1294) show the triumph of the gothic over the classical Roman style as we may see it in the ciboria for instance at Castel S. Elia (Plate 19) near Nepi, at S. Andrea in Flumine, near Ponzano Romano (Plate 22) and in S. Lorenzo fuori le mura (Plate 14) and elsewhere. Decline followed and the school disappears altogether with the departure of the Papal court to Avignon.

I have named as the masterpieces of these *marmorari romani* campanili, cloisters and porticoes, but it is the exquisite decorative works from their hands, the pavements, Paschal candlesticks and Bishops thrones, the ambones and pulpits for which they are most famous.

CAMPANILI

But the artists who made the Cloisters of S. Giovanni in Laterano and S. Paolo fuori le mura at Rome, were more than decorators, they were architects and builders. And it is difficult to deny that it was they who built as well as adorned the exquisite bell towers, the campanili of brick, peculiar to Latium, which are so especially a delight in Rome: the tower of S. Prassede the earliest, the tower of SS. Quattro Coronati of the time of Paschal II so crude still and so strangely set over the central portal of the atrium, that of S. Maria in Cosmedin (Plate 2b) perhaps the most graceful and slender, dating about 1123, that of S. Giorgio in Velabro (Plate 3) so robust and heavy also of the early XIIth century, those of S. Croce in Gerusalemme, SS. Giovanni e Paolo (Plate 1), S. Francesca Romana and S. Pudentiana (Plate 2a) of the middle of the century and those of S. Lorenzo fuori le mura and S. Silvestro in Capite of the end. At Albano, at Velletri, at Tivoli and farther afield at S. Giovanni in Argentella near Palombara, at Montebuono and at Gaeta, to name no others, these lovely Roman towers are to be found.

Did the Roman *marmorari* then indeed construct the buildings they decorated? Were they architects in our sense? Venturi has no doubt of it: "Sumptuous decorators as they are, the Cosmati are first and foremost builders. They balance the masses of their structures with the greatest care and cleverness, and use ornament only to complete the effects of their architectural designs."[1]

[1] A Venturi: *A Short History of Italian Art* (Macmillan 1926).

CLOISTERS

There can be little doubt that they built, they certainly signed, the great cloisters in Rome, and at Subiaco and at Sassovivo.

The earliest of these is the cloister of the SS. Quattro Coronati (Plate 4b) which dates from the early years of the XIIth century. It is unsigned, but was probably the work of Magister Paulus the craftsman of Paschal II who reconstructed the SS. Quattro Coronati in 1112. This simple and beautiful work is of marble. A doorway breaks each of the longer arcaded sides and there is a pier in the middle of each shorter side. The columns are coupled for I think the first time.

The coupled columns appear again in the cloister of S. Cosimato (Plate 4a) reconstructed in brick about the end of the XIIth century. The cloister of S. Lorenzo fuori le mura erected in 1187 by Pope Clement III is a new attempt at elegance, for even the great cloister of S. Cosimato is, in its two hundred and fifty or so columns, very uncertain in workmanship, though perhaps restoration has here something to answer for. The sculptured capitals and workmanship generally in the cloister of S. Sabina, which is a few years later in date, are certainly better.

The first signed cloister is that of S. Scolastica at Subiaco (Plates 5b, 9a) which was the work of generation after generation of the family of Laurentius. Magister Jacobus signed on one side:

MAGISTER IACOBUS ROMAN̄ FECIT HOC O̅P̅

He alternates coupled shafts with single ones, each with its own base. The other three sides date later and are by Jacobus' son and grandsons who sign

COSMAS ET FILII LU̅C̅ ET IA̅C̅ AL̅T̅

ROMANI CIVES IN MARMORIS ARTE PERITI

HOC OPUS EXPLERUNT ABI̅S̅ TP̅E̅ LANDI

It is interesting to see the change and indeed the advance in workmanship very obvious in the work of these three generations.[1]

Is it now, in the cloister begun in 1205 "arte sua" by Peter of Capua, Cardinal and Abbot of S. Paolo fuori le mura (Plates 5a and 9b), we see the influence of the Byzantine school of Palermo and South Italy? Was it he who first began to decorate a cloister with mosaics of porphyry and verde antico in friezes and panels of mosaic? It was in 1205 the construction was begun of the north-east side of the cloister in the time of Peter of Capua (1193-1209). The work continued till 1225 when it was suspended for some years, perhaps because it was then the great mosaic of the apse was remade. The construction of the cloister was resumed and as P. Fedele has established finished before 1235 in a manner very different. Even at a glance it is

[1] Venturi: *Storia dell' Arte Italiana* III, p. 791, note, seems to think that the *IACOBUS* who signed this was the last master to work here: "Rimasto solo Iacobo all' opera". It is however difficult to believe the side signed by *IACOBUS* alone to be later than the rest instead of earlier, moreover *EXPLERUNT* surely means what it says.

easy to see the difference in style between the side next the church and the other three not only in the architecture but in the mosaic and ornament.

The whole work bears this inscription:

HOC OPUS ARTE SUA QUEM ROMA CARDO BEAVIT
NATUS DE CAPUA PETRUS OLIM PRIMITIAVIT
ARDEA QUEM GENUIT QUIBUS ABBAS VIXIT IN ANNIS
CETERA DISPOSUIT BENE PROVIDA DEXTRA IOHANNIS

Between the first side of the cloister here and the first side of the Lateran cloister there is a considerable likeness. It is probable these two sides which are of the same general proportions, were the work of the same architects namely Vassallettus and his son Petrus and it is astonishing that the other three sides of both cloisters, though so different from the earlier sides of each, should so nearly resemble one another, though the Lateran cloister is everywhere the more elaborate and the more beautiful. Peter of Capua and Abbot Iohannes of the inscription almost certainly had no more to do with the actual work that to preside over the building, though possibly Peter was answerable for the Byzantine influence.

This style of decoration with pieces of porphyry and verde antico and mosaic, full of delightful colour, was brought to perfection in the glorious cloister of the Lateran (Plates 6a, 6b, 7a, 7b, 8), the work of Vassalletus and his son who finished it.

NOBILIT DOCT HAC VASSALLECTUS
I ARTE CU PATRE CEPIT OPUS
QD SOL PERFECIT IPE[1]

The cloisters of S. Giovanni and S. Paolo fuori le mura are masterpieces of the cosmatesque style of architecture and decoration. That of S. Giovanni is the finer, the coupled columns of diverse and gracious forms, sometimes straight, sometimes twisted and shining with mosaic are surmounted by an architrave glorious with a frieze of decoration of verde antico and porphyry ornament (Plate 8). Above this is a cornice of sculpture sometimes nearly in the round, with youthful heads so full of animation and character that we realize we have here the work of a new master in Petrus Vassallettus. His are the sphinxes, copies from the antique, which we find at the entry (Plate 7b) and we shall come upon his work again in the Paschal candlestick at S. Paolo (Plates 39, 40a, 40b, 41) and again at Anagni (Plate 43b). Nothing lovelier, not even at Monreale, whose cloister may have inspired this Roman masterpiece, exists anywhere. A classic repose and spirit, Virgilian in its ideal serenity, fill the lovely enclosed space with their own light:

largior hic campos aether et lumine vestit
purpureo, solemque suum, sua sidera norunt. . . .

[1] Cf. G. Giovannoni: *Opere dei Vassalletti Marmorari Romani* in *L'Arte* (1908), pp. 262, et seq. E. Lavagnino *S. Paolo sulla via Ostiense* (Roma 1924) reads *NOBILITATE DOCTUS*. Frothingham: *The Monuments of Christian Rome* (New York, 1908) reads *NOBILITER DOCTUS*. Venturi *op. cit.*, III, p. 789, reads *NOBILIS ET DOCTUS*.

PORTICO AND PORCH

If the cloisters of SS. Quattro Coronati, of S. Scolastica, S. Lorenzo, S. Paolo fuori le mura and S. Giovanni in Laterano were the masterpieces of the school it was hardly less successful in its other achievements such as the porticos of S. Lorenzo fuori le mura (Plate 14), the most classical, S. Giorgio in Velabro (Plate 3), S. Saba. There was also the older porch which may be studied at S. Clemente and S. Cosimato and S. Prassede.

The architraved as opposed to the arcaded portico was characteristic of the "Cosmati" school though the restored porch at S. Maria in Cosmedin is arched (Plate 2b). The architraved portico first appears perhaps at S. Lorenzo in Lucina, but comes to perfection in S. Giorgio in Velabro (Plate 3), S. Crisogono, S. Maria and S. Cecilia in Trastevere, SS. Giovanni e Paolo and at S. Lorenzo fuori le mura (Plate 14) which Vassallettus built and decorated for Honorius III. The most splendid example, however, is that of the Duomo of Città Castellana (Plates 16 and 17) which the "Cosmati", the son and grandson of Laurentius, built in 1210. The curious double portico of S. Saba, signed by Iacobus the son of Laurentius

FACTUM EST P̄ MANUS MAGISTRI IACOBI

is an exceptional work and no longer æsthetically very successful.

The Cathedral of Città Castellana is a basilica of three naves much resembling S. Pietro at Tuscania and S. Maria di Castello at Tarquinia. It has been entirely modernized but the pavement and the façade and portico time has spared and man the destroyer has respected.

The façade, which is earlier than the portico, has a central portal flanked by two others and above a magnificent rose now hidden by the arch (Plates 18 and 17).

The central door is inscribed on the lintel:

LAURENTIUS CUM IACOBO FILIO SUO MAGISTRI DOCTISSIMI ROMANI HOC OPUS
FECERUNT

This portal (Plate 18) is very lovely. It consists of a great round multiple arch supported on either side by a pilaster and two columns. The inner columns stand on two magnificent lions. The sculptured capitals of pilasters and columns are surmounted by a great band of mosaic which stretches across the doorway upon the lintel, and the door itself is framed in a great and beautiful border of cosmatesque mosaic, rectangular pieces and small discs of porphyry purple and green in borders of white marble.

Above the doorway, in the lunette, is a half rose studded with mosaic and about it a border of white marble decorated with a beautiful pattern of porphyry mosaic.

The side door on the gospel side is not decorated, but that on the right (Plate 15a) is encased in marble mosaic and is signed:

M̄A IACŌ + RAINERIUS PETRI
RODOLFI FIERI FECIT + BUS
M̄ FECIT.

This portal under a round arch decorated in mosaic, is itself framed in bands of mosaic and in the lunette is a mosaic of Our Lord in benediction holding a book.

One concludes then, that this beautiful unfinished façade was the work of Laurentius assisted as ever by his son Jacobus, who alone and perhaps later decorated the side door on the right.

But this very lovely façade was entirely hidden and lost when in 1210 the great and even more lovely portico was built with its towering and I think unique triumphal arch (Plates 16, 17).

The façade is thus seen to have been built before 1210 and perhaps a good deal before, if we are right in supposing that Jacobus was a young man when he helped his father Laurentius to build it. Then perhaps after the death of his father he built the side door on the right, but for some reason did not continue with that on the left. As a man well on in years, assisted in his turn by his son Cosmas, he built the portico and triumphal arch eclipsing his father's work and the work of his youth.

The portico stands on a broad platform of eight steps which stretches across the whole front of the church. This serves as its base and greatly adds to the grace and dignity of the whole.

It is divided into two parts, each of four intercolumnar spaces, by the triumphal arch opposite the central portal of the façade. The columns, three on either side, are monoliths standing on simple isolated bases, the capitals as is generally the case in the works of the school are Ionic, surmounted by a sculptured abacus. Large square pillars close the ends of the portico and uphold the triumphal arch. The entablature is of good proportions, though perhaps the architrave is a little too high. The frieze is richly decorated with mosaic. A roof of tiles covers the gallery.

The triumphal arch in the midst is supported by two great square pillars and above the arch itself rises a wall crowned with a mosaic frieze and entablature with a cornice similar to that of the portico. The key of the arch is surmounted by a sculpture in high relief of the Pascal Lamb and in the tympanum are two eagles on brackets. Above the eagle on the left is a cross in mosaic. Beneath the mosaic frieze of the entablature runs the inscription and signature:

MAGISTER IACOBUS CIVIS ROMANUS CUM COSMA FILIO SUO CARISSIMO FECIT HOC OPUS
ANNO DN̄I MCCX[1]

And round the curve of the great arch we read

GLORIA IN EXCELSIS DEO ET IN TERRA PAX HOMINIBUS BONAE VOLUNTATIS

The appearance of this great work is most beautiful, noble and magnificent. The portico and triumphal arch are indeed the work of a mature scholar. They are a

---

[1] Is it possible to conclude that "*FILIO SUO CARISSIMO*" suggests that Cosma was still a very young person, not more than a boy, helping his devoted parent? In a piece of mosaic of the left pilaster of the Triumphal Arch is a fragment of an inscription which E. Stevenson, who first noticed it, completed thus (*Iaco*)*BUS LA*(*ure*)*NTII*. This might suggest that *IACOBUS* began the portico alone and completed it with his son.

resurrection, a renaissance of classical antiquity and the greatest achievement of this sort of the *marmorari romani*.

I have sometimes regretted that the façade with its lovely rose window is now entirely hidden by the triumphal arch with its very awkward gable roof (Plate 17). This arch has about it something almost hysterical, something fantastic, but it is so daring in its backward glance at the ancient world, so touching in its nostalgia, and the portico which it divides is so harmonious and so lovely that any regret is lost in admiration and wonder at finding so strange and so beautiful a vision, a reminiscence of the classical world, in the heart of the Middle Age and in this half forgotten place under Soracte.[1]

At Tarquinia in S. Maria in Castello (Plate 10b) and at S. Pietro at Toscanella (Plate 12, 13a, 13b) too, the Ranucii signed façade and portal. In Rome we have the portals of S. Tommaso in Formis (Plate 15b) and of S. Antonio Abate near S. Prassede, but most of the façades by the Cosmatesque masters, such as those of S. Maria Maggiore, S. Giovanni in Laterano and others have been destroyed. The beautiful portal of S. Tommaso in Formis (Plate 15b) with its round arch of marble signed:

MAGISTER IACOBUS CUM FILIO SUO COSMATO FECIT HOC OPUS

was built in 1218. Above it is a tabernacle, resting upon the arch of the portal itself, under a round arch supported by two columns; within the niche in a round is a mosaic of Our Lord enthroned between a black and a white slave, for the little church was once attached to the Trinitarian Order devoted to the redemption of slaves, and its badge, a red and blue cross, is above.

Such was the achievement of these Roman craftsmen in architecture, but when they devoted themselves to the production of the furniture of the church, magnificent decorators though they proved themselves to be, they did not cease to be architects.

The best example remaining to us of a church of the time of the *marmorari romani* —the XIIth and XIIIth century—of the time that is from Pascal II to Honorius III, is to be found in S. Clemente (Plate 11) which was restored and rearranged, sometimes with older material, by its titular Cardinal, Anastasio, in the first quarter of the XIIth century. ANASTASIUS PRESBITER CARDINALIS HUIUS TITULI HOC OPUS COEPIT ET PERFECIT we read round the circular back of the Bishop's throne. Even here an older piece of marble was adapted. His sepulchral inscription (before 1128) was in the portico of the church.

With S. Clemente should be consulted and compared S. Maria in Cosmedin, which was restored and cleared and rearranged as a church of the XIIth century in 1894-1899. This restoration using the old materials was admirably done, but the upper church of S. Clemente is the more authentic.

[1] Under the portico in 1911 there was preserved a made-up portal—the framing of a doorway from S. Francesco in Città Castellana. This consisted of two pilasters with spiral *scanalatura* and a lintel beautifully decorated in mosaic. It is illustrated by A. Munoz in *Bollettino d'Arte*, 1911, p. 125.

THE CIBORIUM

Certainly of all the furniture of a church of this time the ciborium, the baldacchino, over the altar was the most architectural, its beauty lay not in its decoration but in its structure. Of these ciboria the *marmorari romani* created many masterpieces, from the earlier like those in S. Cesareo and SS. Nereo ed Achilleo and at S. Giovanni in Argentella near Palombara, to the fully developed three-tiered canopy of S. Lorenzo fuori le mura and the magnificent structure in the Duomo of Anagni (Plate 21).

The early ciborium at S. Cesareo of the XIIth century has arches upon its four columns surmounted by a cornice on which rests a triangular tympanum. In SS. Nereo ed Achilleo the ciborium has a cupola. At S. Giovanni in Argentella the earlier type is found with a triangular tympanum upon four arches.

A far lovelier example of the art of the Roman craftsman is to be seen at Castel S. Elia near Nepi (Plate 19), indeed I sometimes think this to be the most perfect of all in its exquisite proportion and simplicity, though perhaps one is influenced by its beautiful setting in the lovely frescoed apse and standing on the magnificent mosaic pavement of this far away and hard to reach monastic church. Upon four columns with sculptured capitals we have, not arches, but four simple classic architraves upon which four small corner columns and three on each side uphold a further four architraves upon which rests a gable roof. A somewhat similar ciborium is in S. Clemente in Rome but it is larger and to my mind far less lovely (Plate 11).

It is at S. Giorgio in Velabro (Plate 20) and at S. Lorenzo fuori le mura that we find in Rome the all but full development of the Roman ciborium of the XIIth century.

Upon the four columns about the altar at S. Giorgio in Velabro rest four architraves decorated with mosaic upon which eight small columns in each side uphold four other architraves upon which small columns arranged in octagonal form uphold a lanterned canopy, the lantern being itself columned. This lovely construction is carried out even more elaborately though not more beautifully in the ciborium of S. Lorenzo fuori le mura, built by the sons of Paulus and signed and dated 1148:

IOHANNES PETRUS ANGELUS ET SASSO
FILII PAULI MARMORARII HUIUS OPERIS
MAGISTRI FUERUNT MCXLVIII

A similar ciborium is to be found at S. Andrea in Flumine near Ponzano Romano (Plate 22). This is earlier and more authentic than that by the same master in S. Maria in Castello at Tarquinia. It is signed:

NICOLAUS CUM SUIS FILIIS IOHN ET GUITTONE FECERUNT HOC OPUS

At S. Maria in Vulturella north-east of Rome in the Aniene, the octagonal arrangement of the canopy begins at once and rests on the first architraves with lantern above.

14

The complicated style reaches its full development and perfection at Anagni (Plate 21) in the XIIIth century where we find a double lantern crowning the structure. This is probably the work of Cosmas who signed the pavement.

The ciborium over the high altar in the Duomo of Ferentino (Plate 23) is a less developed and a less successful work, at least as we have it. It was made by Drudus, who was perhaps a pupil of Cosmas and was associated with Cosmas' son Lucas at Città Castellana as we shall see. He signs the ciborium here at Ferentino:

MAGISTER DRUDUS DE TRIVIO
CIVIS ROMANUS FECIT HOC OPUS

There followed the work of Arnolfo, who, associated as we may believe him to have been with the Roman School, was a Tuscan and enamoured of gothic and then perhaps the influence of the Cistercian Abbeys was too overwhelming for the classic Roman style to maintain itself. However it may have been, the pointed arch appears in the ciboria at S. Paolo fuori le mura and S. Cecilia in Trastavere, the work of Arnolfo, and was imitated at S. Giovanni in Laterano and S. Maria in Cosmedin where the ciborium is signed by Deodatus, who we believe to have been a son of Cosmas II (Cosmatus).

ALTARS

It was ever the custom in Rome to erect a ciborium or canopy over the high altar. The altar itself from being often a table of stone had by edict of Felix I become a tomb or reliquary of the martyrs and it was this which changed the form of the altar from a simple table to that of a sarcophagus, access being given to the relic itself often by raising the altar on a platform or steps, the officiating priest facing the nave as at S. Giorgio in Velabro (Plate 20) for instance, at Anagni (Plate 21), Ferentino (Plate 23) and in many other places where an altar elaborately decorated with mosaics stands under its ciborium above the shrine or reliquary of the saint, equally elaborately decorated with mosaic, to which one descends on either side by a flight of steps into the *confessio*. An example on a grand scale is to be seen at S. Lorenzo fuori le mura and in most of the Basilicas in Rome. The high altar of S. Giorgio in Velabro and also of the Duomo of Ferentino are good examples of this time (Plates 20 and 23). The altar of the latter is typically and beautifully adorned with mosaic: two large monolithic rounds of imperial porphyry on the west front of the altar, set in an intricate pattern of mosaic and supported on either side by twisted marble columns adorned with mosaic. An even more elaborated frontal appears on the high altar in S. Cesareo where the front is panelled: in the centre a large monolithic round of porphyry set in a border of mosaic, flanked on either side by a rectangular oblong panel of porphyry also set in elaborate mosaic borders. A similar altar may be seen in S. Prassede (Plate 24*a*) and in S. Maria Maggiore, in the Altare della Cula (Plate 24*b*). This is flanked by two twisted columns of marble elaborately mosaiced. We have a rather different example at Subiaco (Plate 25) under a gothic canopy. The most splendid of such altars, now restored, must have been the high altar in the lower church of S. Francis at Assisi —an immense *mensa* supported on an arcade of pointed arches all covered with mosaic and supported by columns of various forms. This stands directly over the tomb of S. Francis. Another very beautiful altar in the form of a chest or tomb used to stand in the upper church of S. Francis at Assisi, and this too, in a heavily restored form, may still be seen there in the crossing.

SCREENS

Before and about the altar stood the iconostasis (if in fact an iconostasis it was) and the sanctuary or choir screens. Perhaps the best example of the former *in situ* is to be found in the church of S. Giovanni in Argentella near Palombara Sabina. This is dated 1170

. . . ANNO CENTENO SEPTUAGESIMO ATQUE MILLENO . . .

and fragments of a so-called iconostasis may be seen in S. Alessio in Rome—two beautifully mosaiced columns which are said to have come from S. Bartolommeo all'Isola. But it might seem doubtful whether an iconostasis ever existed in Rome at any rate under the Latin rite and the so-called iconostasis in Central Italy may only be a more elaborate form of choir or sanctuary screen. The iconostasis at S. Giovanni in Argentella near Palombara Sabina consists of magnificently mosaiced panels set up across and before the sanctuary upon which stands a screen of four columns up-holding an architrave.

Of screens the finest examples are those now in the sacristy of the Duomo of Città Castellana (Plate 47) and, with the Bishop's throne in the midst, that of S. Lorenzo fuori le mura (Plate 26) and those in S. Clemente, S. Maria in Cosmedin (reconstructed), S. Sabina (reconstructed), S. Balbina, S. Cesareo, SS. Nereo ed Achilleo in Rome and S. Francesco at Sutri.[1]

The magnificent screens at Città Castellana are supported by pilasters or twisted columns, and have the one two couched lions, the other a lion and sphinx at their base. One is inscribed:

DRUD' ET LUCAS CIVES ROMANI MAGISTRI DOCTISSIMI
HOC OPUS FECERUNT

Clause and Venturi read DEOD ET LUCAS[2]. The Drudus of the above reading is no doubt the Drudus de Trivio who made the ciborium in the Duomo of Ferentino, which he seems to have copied from the work of Cosmas at Anagni and not very successfully. He appears to have been thus a pupil of Cosmas (ca. 1220) and then came to be associated with Cosmas' son Lucas at Città Castellana.

---

[1] Venturi *Op. cit.*, III, p. 778.

[2] G. Clause: *Les Cosmati et S. Marie à Civita Castellana* in *Revue de l'Art Chretien*, 1897, p. 275. Venturi: *Storia dell' Arte Italiana*, III, p. 792, note. There can be no doubt that Clause and Venturi are mistaken, the inscription certainly is Drudus.

THE EPISCOPAL THRONE

Behind the altar and generally in the apse rose the Bishop's throne sometimes set in a marble screen decorated with mosaics as in S. Balbina and S. Lorenzo fuori le mura (Plate 26) where we find the most magnificent panelled screen richly sculptured and set with panels of porphyry in mosaic, in the midst of which is established the round headed Episcopal throne adorned with rounds and squares of porphyry and mosaics and supported by two twisted columns set with mosaics. All is of the XIIth century.

At S. Cesareo (Plate 29*a*) flanked by two heavy twisted columns which have lost their mosaics and which with a heavy architrave under a gable make a sort of canopy, the Episcopal throne with its round head is set, encrusted with porphyry rounds and mosaics which include figure mosaics of birds and an animal.

In the neighbouring church of SS. Nereo ed Achilleo (Plate 28*b*) we find an even more magnificent but later throne with its gothic back covered with mosaic, supported by two columns with twisted *scanalatura,* the throne itself supported by two lions. No doubt this throne with the rest of the church has been considerably restored, if only by Cardinal Baronius in the XVIth century, who left an inscription to the right of the throne imploring his successors—he was titular of the church—not to alter it in any way. It is now (1949) closed and undergoing restoration. The Cardinal also caused to be inscribed, on the back of the Episcopal throne, part of S. Gregory the Great's Homily on SS. Nereo ed Achilleo under the mistaken impression that it had been delivered from this throne in this church, whereas it was really read in the neighbouring catacomb of Domitilla.

Among the other cosmatesque Episcopal thrones in Rome is that in S. Clemente which seems older than the XIIth century, that much restored in S. Sabina (Plate 28*a*), the magnificent but half ruined throne of S. Silvestro (Plate 30*b*) now in the cloister of the Lateran and the glorious throne between four twisted columns with a gothic back all adorned with mosaics in the Grotte Vaticane (Plate 30*a*).

But the most beautiful of all these Episcopal thrones of the "Cosmati" might seem to be that at Anagni (Plate 27), so stately in the dignity of its simplicity and shining with mosaics. It stands on a great marble platform flanked and supported by two lions—the forequarters and head only—between which the simple square cathedra of white marble is established. The back of the throne is a large circular slab of white marble with a six pointed star of two triangles in mosaic and six small rounds of mosaic in the angles. It is signed

VASALETUS DE ROMA ME FECIT

The whole is almost Mycenæan in its majesty.

In the upper church of S. Francesco at Assisi there is an Episcopal throne covered by a canopy (Plate 29*b*). Two lions form the arms of this considerably restored work. At Ferentino and at Fondi too there are thrones, the work of the "Cosmati".

AMBONES

As always it is to S. Clemente and S. Maria in Cosmedin we turn when we seek to know what a church of the time of Pope Pascal II looked like and this is especially true of the church furniture and most of all of the *Ambones* (Plates 31 and 33).

Two *ambones* or pulpits from which the Epistle and Gospel were sung were in the XIIth century usually to be found in the more important churches. Originally there had been only one and that in the nave, with two flights of steps,[1] one from the east and the other from the west. The deacon at the top of the eastern steps with his face to the altar read the epistle, from the top of the western steps facing the people the deacon read the gospel. This single ambone was found to be inconvenient and a second was erected, so that there was one on each side of the choir.

This is what we find more or less in an original state at S. Clemente (Plate 31) and reconstructed and rearranged in S. Maria in Cosmedin (Plate 33). The beautiful and simple but complete ambones with their double flights of steps and *pulpitum* in S. Clemente are probably earlier than the "Cosmati"; they are of marble without mosaic. Those at S. Maria in Cosmedin have a small amount of mosaic in borders beneath the *pulpitum* but are otherwise very similar to those in S. Clemente. The best example of a "Cosmati" ambone is that in S. Lorenzo fuori le mura (Plate 32) which is similar in form to those in S. Clemente and S. Maria in Cosmedin but decorated with magnificent great slabs and rounds of porphyry framed in mosaic. In the pulpitum the reading desk is supported by an eagle, sculptured in the round, of white marble. This may well date from the middle of the XIIth century when the ciborium was made.

The magnificent ambone in S. Maria di Castello at Tarquinia (Plate 35) by Giovanni di Guittone Romano is signed and dates from 1209; it is, however, much reconstructed. Another complete and beautiful work of the XIIIth century was in the church of S. Pietro at Alba Fucense, destroyed by earthquake in 1915.

The ambone in S. Cesareo (Plate 37) is called by Venturi *il più romano tra questi pulpiti*. No doubt that is so in style, but this magnificent work is, as I see it, only a fragment reconstructed, in the Renaissance perhaps, from the original ambone with its two flights of steps. As we have it with its single stairway, its fine sculptures, its twisted columns filled with mosaics, its lovely rounds of imperial porphyry set in mosaic within a carven frame, its sculptured niche beneath the *pulpitum,* it is a ravishing piece of work and if it is a fragment we should be grateful to the Renaissance for having left us so lovely a thing in spite of our regret for what has been destroyed.

It is unquestionably the same with regard to the two ambones of S. Maria in

---

[1] The word Ambo (Ambone) of Greek origin and possibly derived from ἀναβαίνω —I go up, signified according to Innocent III a high place or elevation: for in his work on the Mass (III, xxxiii) apropos of the deacon ascending the ambone to read the gospel he quotes Isaiah XL, 9: "O Zion that bringest good tidings get thee up into the high mountain". He also recalls Our Lord preaching from a mountain (Matt. V, 1-2).

Aracoeli (Plates 34a and 34b), they have at some time or other been dismantled, rebuilt and rearranged. There was originally certainly one double-stepped ambone, while now we have two, each with one flight of steps, and facing differently. However much we may regret this reconstruction what we have is early work, the ambone on the right being signed by Laurentius himself

LAURENTIUS CUM IACOBO FILIO SUO HUIUS OPERIS MAGISTER FUIT

Different in form as they now are we cannot suppose that they were not originally both from the same hand. The Gospel pulpit has, as at S. Lorenzo and elsewhere, a sculptured eagle—but an eagle strangling a serpent—supporting the parapet which is polygonal and formed by panels of white marble with cornice of mosaic divided by simple pilasters. These panels surely come from a monument much older than the XIIth century, indeed their under surface is covered with sculpture of the VIIIth-IXth centuries. The mosaic work here and in the two twisted columns which support the cornice is of the finest quality.

A true pulpitum, so different from an ambone, is to be found at Fondi in the church of S. Pietro (Plate 38). It is a four-sided square construction richly decorated with mosaic standing upon three arches supported by columns which stand upon sculptured lions.

A similar but even finer pulpitum is to be found in the Duomo of Terracina. These pulpits are more like those of Southern Italy and Sicily than those of the Roman masters—more like those marvellous masterpieces at Ravello, Salerno, Sessa Aurunca, Scala and elsewhere in Campania.

Another form, possibly made up, appears in S. Andrea at Orvieto (Plate 36) where we have a pulpit built on high about a column supported by sculptured marble brackets or corbels. The great panels of the pulpitum itself are richly adorned with mosaic patterns. They look like parts of a screen.

Still of another form and enormous in size is the Cosmatesque pulpit in the lower church of St. Francis at Assisi with its twisted columns in the upper storey, its panels of porphyry, its bands of mosaic and carven corbels.

THE PASCHAL CANDELABRUM

Beside the right-hand ambone in the *coro* stood the Paschal Candelabrum for the Paschal Candle. The peculiarly Roman form of the candelabrum was a twisted column decorated with mosaic, a form perhaps not unknown, but extremely unusual in Southern Italy and Sicily.

The South Italian candelabrum was most often a marble column sculptured in high or low relief as at Gaeta and Salerno or for that matter at Palermo.

This form we find in the magnificent candelabrum of S. Paolo fuori le mura (Plate 39, 40, 41) *vera colonna onoraria* as Venturi calls it. It is some six metres in height and entirely sculptured with reliefs which tell the story of the Passion, Resurrection and Ascension of Our Lord.

Divided into various zones by bands on which are cut inscriptions and the signatures of the two *marmorari romani* who executed it, it was completed about 1170. The reliefs with which it is ornamented represent fantastic animals and episodes in the life of Christ from His betrayal to His ascension. The inscriptions are difficult to read but give us the names of the artists:

EGO NICOLAUS DE ANGILO CUM PETRO BASSALECTO HOC OPUS C̄OPLEVI

and the purpose and use of the Paschal candle is recalled:

ARBOR POMA GERIT—ARBOR EGO LUMINA
GESTO PORTO LIBAMINA—NUNTIO
GAUDIA SED DIE FESTO SURREXIT
CHRISTUS—NAM TALIA NUMERA PST (PRAESTO?)

The candelabrum or column now in the Duomo of Gaeta is a rather gross piece of work, three and a half metres in height decorated with forty-eight reliefs, in twelve verticle zones of four divisions, of scenes in the life of Christ from the Annunciation to the Last Judgment and scenes from the legend of S. Erasmo. The lions upon which it stands do not belong to it. This too is a work of the XIIth century, but not of the Roman school. The candelabrum of S. Paolo is unique as a work of the Roman *marmorari*.

Perhaps the oldest Paschal candelabrum that we know is that in the Duomo of S. Maria della Pietà at Cori (Plate 42*a*). This dates from the first years of the XIIth century. It consists of a cluster of four columns with twisted *scanalatura*, standing on two chimæras, above which is a cylindrical drum carved in relief with animals and stars. The capitals of the columns in relief support a square sculptured block on which stands the large saucer or vase from which the Paschal candle rises. We have no clue to the authorship of this early candelabrum, which is I think unique of its kind in the province of the Roman *marmorari*.

The "Cosmati" as a rule confined themselves to a form of candelabrum which was peculiarly their own. It consisted of a twisted column of marble adorned with mosaic crowned with a capital bearing saucer or vase of classic form from which rose the Paschal candle. Possibly, this form was copied from those candelabra which had been found in the Pagan temples and brought almost as trophies into the Christian churches. We may find two of them in the Vatican Museum.

Such candelabra may be seen in S. Clemente (Plate 31) in S. Maria in Cosmedin (Plate 33) where the column is supported by a couchant lion and in other churches in Rome, for instance in S. Lorenzo fuori le mura (Plate 32) and SS. Nereo ed Achilleo. That in S. Cecilia in Trastevere is attributed to Arnolfo.

But the finest examples are to be looked for outside Rome in Anagni, in Ferentino, at Vulturella and Terracina.

The finest of these is perhaps the magnificent Paschal candlestick in the Duomo at Anagni signed VASSALLETUS ME FECIT (Plates 43*a* and 43*b*). It stands on two sphinxes and consists of a great twisted column decorated with mosaic, crowned with a flat plinth on which half kneels on a serpent a figure of a child in the round, upholding on his head with his two hands the sculptured cup from which the Paschal candle is to rise. Unfortunately the mosaic is almost entirely a restoration of 1904.

The largest of these Paschal candelabra is that in the Duomo of Ferentino (Plate 42b), it is some twenty-five feet in height. It rises from a circular base and is crowned with a mosaiced cup standing on circular carved and mosaiced rounds as pedestals. Much of the marble mosaic in the lower part of the twisted column has perished. These mosaics of marble tesserae both here and at Anagni are earlier than the glass mosaics which after the first third of the XIIIth century were in general use for the purposes of decoration.

The magnificent and elaborate candelabrum in the Duomo of Terracina (Plate 44) is of this sort. It dates about 1245. The great twisted column adorned with glass mosaic stands on a lofty base on which two lions are couched; they bear the square block from which rises the twisted column on its circular base. It is crowned with a Corinthian capital upon which from a square plinth adorned with mosaic, rises the classic vase or cup from a ball on an octagonal base, all ornamented with mosaic. This lovely and elaborated work is attributed to the Roman masters on the verge of their territory.

TOMBS

The cosmatesque tombs in Rome are difficult to date in their proper order. All seem to belong to the second half of the XIIIth century except that of Cardinal Aquasparta in S. Maria in Aracoeli which is dated 1304; but as one dates the others according to the year in which the occupant of the tomb died, many of them may even be as late as the early part of the XIVth century. The earliest is almost certainly that of Cardinal Fieschi in S. Lorenzo fuori le mura (Plate 48), and it is a most typical cosmatesque funeral monument. It is surmounted by what might appear to be the front of a ciborium in which two columns with Ionic capitals support an architrave decorated with a mosaic border on which stands a number of small columns, which support a cornice adorned with a band of mosaic over which in the midst is a squared pillar upholding the gable canopy; all precisely as we find in the ciboria of the school. Beneath is an antique pagan sarcophagus sculptured with a nuptial scene, with Juno and Hymen, in high relief and, above, the Dioscuri and the Infernal divinities, and Day and Night. Above the sarcophagus is a fresco of Our Lord enthroned with SS. Ippolito and Lorenzo who present Pope Innocent IV whose nephew Cardinal Fieschi was, and the Cardinal himself.

Venturi regards the fact that the Cardinal was buried in an antique sarcophagus as a proof of the poverty of invention of the *marmorari romani*, but it might seem more likely that it was the dead man himself who had chosen so splendid a resting place. The horror of paganism was no longer valid in the Renaissance of the XIIth and XIIIth century. We find a similar sarcophagus chosen to hold the remains of Luca and Antonio Savelli in S. Maria in Aracoeli (Plate 49). Here too we have a canopy borne by two marble columns and beneath this, imposed upon a pagan sarcophagus with Bacchus and his rout in high relief, is a sarcophagus of marble between two buttresses all decorated with mosaics and coats of arms, above which is a small frontal or façade with a gothic gable in which is a small rose and beneath in a niche the Madonna and Child enthroned. But the whole monument no longer belongs to the XIIIth century, it has been remade at a later date.

The monument of Pope Honorius IV also in S. Maria in Aracoeli (Plate 52) is similar in style and of about the same date (the Pope died in 1281), but without the pagan sarcophagus, which may be said to support the claim that it was not the "Cosmati" who chose such a sepulchre for these princes of the Church. But here again in the tomb of Honorius we have a canopy upheld by two marble columns which rest upon a platform beautiful with mosaic. On this platform the sarcophagus, richly ornamented with mosaic and adorned with coats of arms, stands bearing the effigy of the Pope somewhat awkwardly reclined upon his pillows, but nevertheless with great dignity, fully vested and wearing the tiara. The cosmatesque tomb of Cardinal Anchero of Troyes, a Frenchman, in S. Prassede is of the same time.

With the tomb of Cardinal Guglielmo Durante in S. Maria sopra Minerva (he died in 1296) we come upon the gothic development here in Rome for the first time. It was then becoming the accepted form.

The figure of the Cardinal lies upon a sarcophagus sculptured with rich cloths and ornamented with coats of arms on a mosaic background. Over all rises a gothic canopy decorated with mosaic and within it a cosmatesque mosaic of the Madonna and Child enthroned between two saints who present the Cardinal to Our Lady. The tomb is the work of Giovanni Cosmati and is signed:

IOHS FILIUS MAGRI COSMATI FEC HOC OP

The sudden change to the gothic manner and form so foreign to the Cosmatesque style as we know it till now, is probably due to the influence of Arnolfo who was the elder contemporary of Giovanni and Deodato Cosmati. Giovanni Cosmati is chiefly known by his sepulchral monuments. He signed again the equally gothic tomb of Cardinal Consalvo Rodriquez (d. 1299) in S. Maria Maggiore (Plate 53) for which he also made a mosaic of Our Lady enthroned with her little Son between two saints:

HOC OP FEC IOHES FILIUS MAGRI COSME CIVIS ROMANUS

And again in S. Balbina we find his work in the spoiled tomb of Cardinal de Surdis (d. 1302) with the arms of the Cardinal in mosaic, white on a blue ground:

+ IOHS FILIUS MAGRI COSMATI FECIT HOC OPUS

And yet again we find him in S. Maria in Aracoeli, for the tomb of Cardinal Matteo d'Acquasparta though it is not signed, is surely his work.

All these gothic tombs are of the same design having a double base on which the sarcophagus stands, the figure of the deceased lying in repose upon a cloth which falls in folds before the coffin. Above, an angel, or two angels, draws aside a curtain. Over all is a gothic canopy beneath which is a mosaic or fresco generally of Our Lady enthroned with patron saints who present the deceased to Her and Her

Son. The design and the workmanship are poor, the sculpture lifeless. The best of the mosaics is that over the tomb of Guglielmo Durante in S. Maria sopra Minerva. Was it perhaps Giovanni[1] who made the tombstone with its mosaic of the Dominican General Muñoz de Zamora in the pavement of the church of S. Sabina?

Outside Rome Cosmati tombs are rare, and it is really only at Viterbo, Anagni, Assisi and Westminster Abbey we find them at all.

In the church of S. Francesco at Viterbo are three cosmatesque tombs, that of Pope Clement IV (d. 1268) that of Peter de Vico (d. 1268) and that of Pope Hadrian V (d. 1276).

The tomb of Pope Clement IV (d. 1268) signed by Petrus Oderisi: PETRUS ODERISI SEPULCRI FECIT HOC OPUS (Plates 51 and 50) is thought to have been the first sepulchral monument to exhibit both sculpture and mosaic and it is possible that we have here the first example of the gothic style, the pointed arch displacing the architrave and the classic order. At the foot of the Pope's tomb is that of his nephew Pierre le Gros. Both Pope and nephew were French and Frothingham suggests that it is here we may find the reason for the sudden introduction of the gothic style into Roman art. He thinks it came from France and is due to this French Pope and the Archbishop of Narbonne who had the ordering of the monument.[2] If that is so it had a very far reaching influence, for not only are the tombs here of Hadrian V and Peter de Vico gothic, but those we have already examined in Rome in S. Balbina (1300), S. Maria sopra Minerva (1296) in S. Maria in Aracoeli (1304), and in S. Maria Maggiore (1299). Moreover it was not long before the ciboria too were to be built in the gothic style as at S. Maria in Cosmedin and elsewhere in Rome. The gothic influence seems more likely to be due to Arnolfo or the Cistercians.

The Petrus Oderisi who made the tomb of Pope Clement IV in Viterbo is said, though uncertainly, to be the craftsman whom Abbot Ware brought from Italy to England on behalf of King Henry III intent on erecting a shrine for the body of St. Edward Confessor in the Abbey Church at Westminster which he was then rebuilding. There are some six cosmatesque works at Westminster and two of them are signed and dated. The pavement in the sanctuary is signed and dated thus:

+ XRI MILLENO BICETENO DUODENO CUM SEXAGENO SUBDUCTUS QUATUOR ANNO TERTIUS HENRICUS REX URBS ODERICUS ET ABBAS HOS COMPEGERE PORPHYREOS LAPIDES.

The inscription ascribes the authorship of this pavement to one Odericus and establishes the date of its making as 1268. Frothingham[3] and others who have followed

---

[1] Could it have been he who made the older parts of the sculptured monuments of Cardinal Guissano da Milano in S. Giovanni in Laterano? Did he or Deodato his brother make that votive group of which only the kneeling figure of Nicholas IV remains to us, also in S. Giovanni in Laterano? The Pope was represented kneeling before the figures of St. Peter and St. Paul, of which figures large fragments remain in the cloister.

[2] Frothingham: *The Monuments of Christian Rome* (New York), 1908, p. 242.

[3] Frothingham: *Op. cit.*, pp. 383-4.

him, would identify the Odericus of the Westminster pavement with the Petrus Oderisi of the tomb of Clement IV in Viterbo. It may be so, though Petrus Oderisi must at this very time have been busy in Viterbo. The late Professor Lethaby however explained the matter as follows: Odericus was not the Petrus Oderisi of the Viterbo tomb, but his father and he concludes that: "Henry III advised by the Pope through Abbot Ware attracted the father (Odericus) to Westminster. The Pope (Clement IV) died in 1268 while Odericus was away from Rome and Peter his son made the Papal tomb. When that was done Peter came to Westminster to execute the basement of the Confessor's Shrine."

This is of course pure conjecture. We know nothing of the author of the two pavements, the shrine, the tomb of King Henry III, the tomb of the young Princes John and Alfonso and of Katherine daughter of Henry III and the tomb slabs of John and Margaret de Valence—all cosmatesque works in the Confessor's Chapel and the Abbey sanctuary. But the shrine at Westminster does show a certain resemblance to the tomb at Viterbo so that it is possible they are by the same master. Even in the tomb of Henry III (Frontispiece) which is undoubtedly by the master who made the shrine, there are likenesses in the mosaic work, but that is not at all decisive, as such mosaic work and its patterns were repeated over and over again.

We have seen that the pavement of the Sanctuary was signed and dated Odericus 1268 (Plate 63). The shrine, now a mere stump, on the other hand was once signed and dated Petrus Romanus Civis 1269 as follows:

(1) ANNO MILENO DOMINI CUM SEXAGENO[1] ET

(2) BIS CENTENO CUM COMPLETO QUASI DENO HOC OPUS EST FACTUM QUOD PETRUS

(3) DUXIT IN ACTUM ROMANUS CIVIS HOMO

(4) CAUSAM NOSCERE SI VIS REX FUIT HENRICUS SANCTI PRESENTIS AMICUS

King Henry died in 1272 and his glorious tomb with its gilt bronze effigy may have been begun before his death. If the reading 1269 instead of 1279 is accepted for the shrine it may have been undertaken immediately after the completion of the shrine to which the body of S. Edward was translated in 1269.

The tomb itself is very Roman and in no way Gothic. It consists of two marble chests superimposed, the lower being the larger. Both were richly adorned with mosaic. The lower chest is supported by pilasters, the upper by twisted columns at the corners. The lower chest is decorated with two squares and a round of green

[1] Sporley's M.S. (1460) as quoted by Lethaby reads *SEPTUAGENO*. Widmore and Neale read *SEXAGENO*. See W. R. Lethaby: *Westminster Abbey and the King's Craftsmen* (London, 1906). The earlier date would seem the more probable considering the date of the sanctuary pavement and the fact that the body of S. Edward was translated to the shrine in 1269. Henry III died 1272. It is very probable that he had his tomb built during his lifetime by the craftsmen from Italy who were at work here, partly for that purpose we may be sure, in 1268. It is hardly likely that the Shrine, the principal work, was only made eleven years after the Sanctuary pavement and ten years after the translation of the body of the Saint.

porphyry, all set in mosaic most of which has disappeared. The upper chest has a magnificent slab of imperial purple porphyry also set in rich mosaic. Upon this upper chest is laid the gilded bronze figure of the King. In the lower chest on the south (or Chapel) side are three niches and here is the only gothic touch in the whole monument for two of them may be said to have what amounts to trefoil arches.

The great monolithic slabs of porphyry must have been brought over the Alps from Italy together with all the other marbles and tesserae. They are still, I believe, the largest monoliths of porphyry in this country, for all imperial purple porphyry as well as all green porphyry is antique. The lost Roman quarries discovered by the late William Brindley in Egypt in the end of the last century,[1] have never been re-opened and worked, so that all the porphyry in the world dates at latest from the time of Justinian, if as late as that (VIth century). No doubt the fact that all the marble for Westminster had to be brought from Italy explains the fact that in the great sanctuary pavement (Plate 63), unlike other Cosmati pavements, there are no large monolithic rounds of porphyry or verde antico or any other marble. Their place is taken at Westminster by mosaic perhaps because the weight of the marbles necessary for monolithic rounds and discs, and perhaps the risk of fracture, would have been too great.

The tomb of the young Princes, John, Alfonso and Katherine, the King's daughter, is also a cosmatesque work. It was removed from the Confessor's Chapel to its present position in the ambulatory, in 1394, to make room for Richard II's tomb. It was made about 1270. The front is divided into two bays and flanked by panelled pilasters once shining with mosaics: the ends were similar. The top of the tomb has a beautiful design of marble rounds down the centre, flanked on either side by rounds filled with small tesserae, the whole richly set in mosaic.

The two grave stones in front of Henry V's tomb are memorials of John and Margaret son and daughter of William de Valance. Of these one was set with mosaic and had an inscription. They form part of the pavement of the Chapel of St. Edward.

PAVEMENTS

We have now to consider the cosmatesque mosaic pavements and I will deal with the two at Westminster first. They are not very characteristic, for as we have seen, and for good reason, they lack the great monoliths, round and rectangular, of porphyry or verde antico, which are so splendid a feature of the cosmatesque pavements of Italy. More, the framework of the Westminster pavements is not of white marble but of the grey-green Purbeck "marble", a very different thing, which damp too easily disintegrates. Glass mosaic also in place of marble seems to have been used in these pavements, and, possibly at a later time, brass has been used for, or to restore, the lettering of the inscriptions. Nothing like this occurs in Italy. The

[1] See *An Unknown Victorian* by Edward Hutton in *The Nineteenth Century and After*, Jan. 1934.

design, however, is extremely fine[1]—super-imposed squares, as in one of the designs in the pavement of the main nave of the Lateran, which I used for the pavement of the Sanctuary of Buckfast Abbey.[2] This Westminster pavement had an inscription which signed and dated the work. ODERICUS (1268), the rest being a rebus in which the day of the Last Judgment might be discovered. (See Index of Places, under London.) The whole pavement is in a deplorable condition.

The pavement in S. Edward's Chapel is now fragmentary but it is I am convinced, an Italian work and not as has been suggested an English attempt at imitation. It resembles the pavements at Farfa (Plate 62) and Terracina, and up and down Latium there are many other pieces of mosaic pavement which are not unlike it.

The remains of another of these cosmatesque pavements may still be seen in Canterbury Cathedral before the place where the shrine of S. Thomas used to stand. (Plate 64). It seems to have been laid down before the altar of the shrine and must date between 1268 and 1278. Much of what remains in the central parts is original and in fair condition; but the mosaic in the semi-circular panels outside the larger square frame and that in the panels in the angles within this frame are not of porphyry purple and green as in the other parts and are modern work probably of the middle of the nineteenth century, and laid much too tight.

To the beautiful Roman pavements I wish I might devote a whole book instead of a few paragraphs as here. I have loved and studied them for fifty years and even now would go a day's journey to see one unknown to me. It is a pity so few have been photographed and that one has to rely on one's sketch book or one's memory to recall them in their various loveliness.

In pagan antiquity the pavement of Basilica, Temple and dwelling had been one of the chief decorative crafts and had come to magnificent perfection as may be seen not only in Rome and Italy but all over the Empire and even in Britain (S. Albans for instance) the last and farthest of the provinces. These pavements more often than not were pictorial and the Christians inevitably imitated them as we may see not only in the Catacombs but outside and now best perhaps at Aquileia where in the area of the Duomo a pavement was brought to light in which, amid the decoration, we see the Good Shepherd with the lamb on his shoulders and the *zampogna* in his hand; small genii are there too, naked or clothed, and on another side the sea monster spues up Jonah in a vast sea of fishes.

But later these pictorial pavements cease to be designed[3] and a great pavement such as that of S. Pietro at Tuscania is made almost without ornament simply with pieces of coloured marble as in the subterranean church of S. Clemente in Rome.

It is at Ravenna however, the centre of Byzantine art in Italy, that in the VIth

[1] Malcolm (1803) describes this pavement as "the most glorious work in England, venerable through age, costly in its materials and invaluable for its workmanship".

[2] See E. Hutton: *The New Pavement in the Sanctuary of Buckfast Abbey* in *Buckfast Abbey Chronicle*, Vol. XIII (1943), pp. 108-9.

[3] The magnificent figured pavement in S. Maria del Patir near Rossano in Calabria is of the twelfth century, but it is a Byzantine work, carried out by and for Greek monks. Cf. P. Orsi: *Le Chiese Basiliane della Calabria* (Florence 1929), pp. 113 *et seq.*

century we find mosaic pavements full of rich colours and accurate workmanship, such as the pavement from S. Apollinare in Classe now in the museum of Ravenna. This is wholly Byzantine of the golden age, entirely geometrical in design and containing nearly all, or almost all, the elements that were to come to such magnificent perfection later. What could be more classical and Roman than the central panel, what more Byzantine than the rest?

But it is in the oratory of S. Zenone in S. Prassede in Rome that at last and in the IXth century we find the great disc or round of porphyry set in a mosaic of porphyry and serpentine and bianco antico, that *opus alexandrinum,* so simple, so lovely, that was to come to its perfection in the art of the "Cosmati".

And with the XIIth century these masters of decoration appear, their technique derived from Byzantine art as we see it at Palermo.

Their work was polychrome and consisted in a geometrical design, a framework, generally of white marble, filled in with great rounds or discs of coloured marble, generally porphyry, set with mosaics of coloured marble *tesserae,* of various sizes and shapes, fitted together in wonderful geometrical patterns, within the great design. This material, mostly porphyry, purple and green, and verde antico was taken from the antique ruins of the classical world and sawn up into pieces of various size. Magnificent examples of such pavements may be seen in Rome, in S. Clemente (Plate 11), S. Maria in Cosmedin (Plates 33 and 54), S. Crisogono, SS. Quattro Coronati, S. Giovanni in Laterano (Plates 56 and 57), S. Maria Maggiore (Plate 58), S. Croce in Gerusalemme, S. Marco, S. Maria in Aracoeli (Plate 59), S. Lorenzo fuori le mura, S. Maria in Trastevere, SS. Nereo ed Achilleo and other churches; and outside Rome at Tarquinia, Anagni (Plate 60), Ferentino, S. Andrea in Flumine, Città Castellana, Farfa (Plates 61 and 62), Castel S. Elia, indeed all over Latium, and even in Umbria in SS. Severino e Martirio in Orvieto and in the Duomo of Spoleto and in Tuscany at Pisa and Lucca.

All these pavements consist in a geometrical design, a framework of white marble, filled in with various geometrical patterns of coloured marble mosaic. And often they show a series of rounds linked or connected by spirals (S. Clemente, Plate 11); of squares of framework superimposed diagonally upon or within one another as in the Lateran (Plate 5), Westminster Abbey (Plate 63); of triangles, of stars or of rectangular forms, oblong or square set in mosaic patterns. Sometimes, as in S. Maria Maggiore (Plate 48) for instance, a whole series of lovely panels is found, each with its own geometrical shape and mosaic pattern.

Some of these works are signed or assignable to definite craftsmen. In the Duomo of Anagni (Plate 60) it is COSMAS CIVIS ROMANUS CUM FILIIS SUIS LUCA ET IACOBO who are the craftsmen; in the Duomo of Ferentino it is PAULUS OPIFEX MAGNUS; at Tarquinia IOHANNES ET GUITTO MAGISTRI of the family of the Ranucii; in the Duomo of Città Castellana it is LAURENTIUS CUM IACOBO FILIO SUO; at the Badia di Farfa (Plates 61 and 62) it is RAINALDUS; at S. Pietro at Alba Fucense the Maestri Romani IOHANNES ET ANDREAS.

If we compare these pavements with those in the Cappella Palatina at Palermo, certainly the finest of the kind in Sicily, we shall see at once that while the technique is the same, the style and the design are quite different, even more in spirit than in form, though that is different enough. One feels before the Palermo pavement with its curiously sharp, acute and sudden angles in the presence of the Orient.[1] On the other hand the "Cosmati" pavements are unmistakably Roman, not Byzantine, and glorify the many basilicas and churches which possess them.

In Rome the pavement in S. Lorenzo fuori le mura is exceptional in that it has a figured panel in the midst. The great pavement of S. Maria Maggiore (Plate 58) with its many panels is a restoration, indeed the whole pavement was relayed in the time of Pope Benedict (ca. 1750). In S. Maria in Aracoeli the cosmatesque work is mixed up with more ancient remnants; this is also the case in S. Cesareo. One of the best, perhaps the latest of these pavements is in the Sancta Sanctorum Chapel at the top of the Scala Santa, the work probably of Cosmas II.

The pavements in S. Maria in Cosmedin have undergone restoration with the rest of the Church (Plates 33 and 54): one of them is signed ALFANUS FIERI TIBI FECIT VIRGO MARIA. The design of discs of porphyry is similar to that in the pavement of the Duomo of Ferentino.

In the great pavement in the nave of S. Giovanni in Laterano several ancient designs of very great beauty may still be seen (Plates 56 and 57).[2]

[1] It was an adaptation of one of the pavements in the Cappella Palatina that was laid down under my direction in St. Paul's Chapel in Westminster Cathedral. I used only Pentelic white marble, porphyry purple and green and verde antico. It is unwise to introduce other colours into these pavements, though the "Cosmati" used sometimes a yellow marble in the smaller tesserae, as at Città Castellana and elsewhere.

[2] The two magnificent designs illustrated in Plates 56 and 57 I repeated in the two pavements, in the Sanctuary and in the crossing under the central Tower, in Buckfast Abbey. The pavement in the Sanctuary (1942-3) is an adaptation of the pavement in the Lateran nave, shown in Plate 57. The colouring I used at Buckfast is white Istrian marble, purple and green porphyry, verde antico, cipollino and Egyptian onyx (a honey-coloured half-transparent alabaster). This pavement at Buckfast is very much larger in scale than its prototype in the Lateran. Unfortunately pieces of porphyry large enough for the great discs or rounds at the four corners that should have been monoliths were not to be had and these rounds had to be made up of smaller pieces which Messrs. Fenning of Hammersmith, marble merchants and contractors, cunningly joined together. In the great central round I substituted a monolith of verde antico for porphyry for this reason. These great rounds are not in the Lateran design and I omitted too the small rounds filled with stars in the four triangles of the design and allowed these triangular panels to remain wholly in mosaic: both these departures from the Lateran design are, I think, to the advantage of the much larger Buckfast pavement. (See E. Hutton: *The New Pavement in the Sanctuary of Buckfast Abbey* in *Buckfast Abbey Chronicle*, Vol. XIII (1943), pp. 107-113.)

In the pavement under the central tower at Buckfast the design is taken from another in the Lateran nave (Plate 56), but is again far larger in scale. Much of the mosaic of the design was replaced by slabs of cipollino for the sake of economy. The border I intended had to be dropped and the Latin inscription I chose in honour of Our Lady, in whose honour the church is dedicated, has not been carried out in the Roman lettering I had had copied from the beautiful inscription in mosaic of S. Sabina in Rome, but in a sort of Byzantine lettering little consistent with the essentially Roman design and character of the pavement. I much regret this, but was not able to prevent it.

These pavements did not, like the rest of the "Cosmati" work, cease to be made when the school came to an end with the departure of the Papacy to Avignon. Even in the Renaissance they were still being composed and by the same methods and with the same technique—as we may see for instance in the Sistine Chapel in the Vatican and elsewhere. Of all the endeavour of the *marmorari romani* it was the pavement alone which remained;—a legacy, as it were of the lovely art to which this essay would be a tribute and of which the plates are in some sort a record.

LIST OF SIGNED INSCRIPTIONS
UNDER ARTISTS' NAMES

The *marmorari romani* were somewhat lavish with their signatures but seldom added the date of their work.

Works no longer in existence are in square brackets.

LIST OF SIGNED INSCRIPTIONS
UNDER ARTISTS' NAMES

PAULUS

    FERENTINO: DUOMO.

       Screen.

       HOC OPIFEX MAGNUS FECIT VIR NOMINE PAULUS . . . PRESUL ERAT SUMMUS
          PASCHALIS PAPA SECUNDUS (1100-1118).

    [ROME: S. Lorenzo fuori le mura.

       Portal.

       PAULUS HES . . . ET FILIPPUS FILIUS EIUS FECERUNT HOC OPUS.]

       Reported by A. Eclissi: *Pitture della basilica di S. Lorenzo* (1639) quoted
          by C. Giovannoni in *L'Arte* 1908, p. 271.

PAULUS AND NICOLAUS SON OF ANGELUS

    ROME: S. Paolo fuori le mura.

       Candelabrum.

       EGO NICOLAUS DE ANGILO CUM PETRO BASSALECTO HOC OPUS COPLEVI.

PAULUS' SONS

    [ROME: S. Bartolommeo all' Isola.

       Inscription in crypt.

       NICOLAUS DE ANGELO FECIT HOC OPUS.]

    [ROME: S. Croce in Gerusalemme.

       Ciborium.

       IOHES DE PAULO CUM FRIB SUIS ANGELO ET SASSO HUIUS OP MAGISTRI
          FUERUNT MCXLIII.]

    [ROME: S. Giovanni in Laterano.

       Ancient Portico.

       NICOLAUS ANGELI FECIT HOC OPUS.]

    ROME: S. Lorenzo fuori le mura.

       Ciborium.

       +IOHS PETRUS ANGELUS ET SASSO FILII PAULI MARMORARII HUIUS OPERIS
          MAGISTRI FUERUNT MCXLVIII.

    ROME: S. Marco.

       Ciborium.

       +IOHS PETRUS ANGELUS SASSO FILII PAULI HUIUS OPERIS MAGISTRI
          FUERUNT.

[SUTRI: Duomo.
High Altar.

HOC OPUS FECIT NICOLAUS ET FILIUS EIUS ANNO INCAR MCLXX.]

Ughelli: *Italia sacra.*

RANUCIUS OR RAINERIUS

ALBA FUCENSE: (destroyed in earthquake of 1915).
Ambone (preserved in a shelter).

CIVIS ROMAN DOCTISSIMUS ARTE IOHS CUI COLLEGA BONUS ANDREAS
DETULIT HONUS HOC OPUS EXCELSUM STRUSSERUNT MENTE PERITI
NOBILIS ET PRUDENS ODERISIUS ABFUIT ABAS.

FONDI: Duomo.
Ambone.

TABULA MARMOREA VITREIS DISTINCTA LAPILLIS DOCTORIS STUDIO SIC EST
ERECTA IOHANNIS ROMANO GENITO COGNOMINE NICOLAO.

Frothingham: *The Monuments of Christian Rome* (New York, 1908),
p. 362, doubts this Nicolaus being of the Ranuci family. Perhaps
Nicholaus de Angelo.

PONZANO ROMANO: S. Andrea in Flumine.
Ciborium.

NICOLAUS CUM SUIS FILIIS IOHANNES ET GUITTONE FECERUNT HOC OPUS.

Ambone also inscribed and dated 1209.
Iohannes, son of Guitto.

. . . A.D. MCCVIIII . . . INNOCEN PP III . . . HOC UP . . . PER MANUS
IOHANNIS GUITTONIS CIVIS RMN.

[ROME: S. Silvestro in Capite.
In a window.

EGO RAINERIUS CUM FILIIS MEIS NICOLAUS ET PETRUS HOC INCIPIMUS ET
COMPLEVIMUS.]

cf. *Arch. della Soc. Rom. di St. Pat.* 1880, p. 375.

TARQUINIA: S. Maria di Castello.
Porta Principale signed on arch:
PETRUS RANUCII.

On architrave:

RANUCII PETRUS LAPIDUM NON DOGMATE MERUS ISTUD OPUS MIRE
STRUXIT QUOQUE FECIT OPTIME MCXLIII.

On window above:

NICOLAUS RANUCII MAGISTER ROMANUS FECIT.

Ciborium.

> JOHANNES ET GUITTO MAGISTRI HOC OPUS FECERUNT MCLXVI.

Ambone.

> HOC OP NITIDUM AURO ET MARMORE DIVERSO FIERI FECIT . . . PER MANUS
> MAGISTRI IOHS GUITTONIS CIVIS RMN.

[TUSCANIA. (TOSCANELLA) S. Maria.
    Facade: On Arch of Portal.
    RANIERI IHIS PERUSINUS.
    In upper window:
    NICOLAUS RANUCIUS CIV MAGISTER ROMANUS FECIT.]
    Reported by Promis: *Notizie Epigrafiche*, p. 7.

(COSMATI) LAURENTIUS AND IACOBUS

CIVITÀ CASTELLANA: Duomo.
    Central Portal.

> + LAURENTIUS CUM IACOBO FILIO SUO MAGISTRI DOCTISSIMI ROMANI H
> OPUS FECERUNT.

FALLERI: S. Maria di Falleri.
    Portal.

> LAURENTIUS CUM IACOBO FILIO SUO FECIT HOC OPUS.

[ROME: S. Apostoli.
    Tabernacle.

> LAURENTIUS CUM IACOBO FILIO SUO HUIUS OPERIS MAGISTRI.]

"Nel 1162 la Basilica si arricchi d'un nuovo Ciborio scolpito da
    Lorenzo di Tebaldo capostitile dei Cosmati." P. Fr. Santilli O.M.
    Conv. *La Basilica dei SS. Apostoli*. (Le Chiese di Roma illustrate)
    (Rome 1925.)

ROME: S. Maria in Aracoeli.
    Ambone.

> LAURENTIUS CUM IACOBO FILIO SUO HUIUS OPERIS MAGISTER FUIT.

[ROME: S. Pietro in Vaticano.
    Pulpit.

> + HOC OPUS EX AURO VITREIS LAURENTIUS EGIT CUM IACOBO NATO
> SCULPSIT SIMUL ATQUE PEREGIT OPUS MAGISTRI VASSALETI QUOD IPSE
> FECIT.]
    Cf. G. Giovannoni in *L'Arte* 1908, p. 280.

SUBIACO: Sacro Speco.
    Portal.

> + SIT PAX INTRANTI SIT GRATIA DIGNA PPECANTI + LAURENTIUS CUM
> IACOBO FILIO SUO FECIT HOC OPUS.

(COSMATI) IACOBUS.

CIVITÀ CASTELLANA: Duomo.

Portal on Right.

M̅A IA̅C̅O̅ + RAINERIUS PETRI RODULFI FIERI FECIT + BUS M. FECIT.

ROME: S. Alessio.

Two small columns from an iconostasis.

+ IACOBUS LAURENTII FECIT HAS DECEM ET NOVEM COLUMPNAS CUM CAPITELLIS SUIS.

ROME: S. Saba.

Portal.

+ HOC OPUS DN̅O̅ IOHANNE ABBATE BENE FACTUM EST P. MANUS MAGISTRI IACOBI +.

SUBIACO: S. Scholastica.

Cloister.

MAGISTER IACOBUS ROMA̅N̅ FECIT HOC O̅P̅.

(COSMATI) IACOBUS CUM COSMA

CIVITÀ CASTELLANA: Duomo.

Triumphal Arch.

MAGISTER IACOBUS CIVIS ROMANUS CUM COSMA FILIO SUO CARISSIMO FECIT OHC OPUS ANNO DN̅I̅ MCCX.

ROME: S. Tommaso in Formis.

Portal.

MAGISTER IACOBUS CUM FILIO SUO COSMATO FECIT HOC OPUS.

(COSMATI) COSMAS

ANAGNI: Duomo.

Pavement.

MAGISTER COSMAS HOC OP FECIT.

ANAGNI: Duomo. Museum.

Pavement.

ANNO DOMINI MCCXXXI PER MANUS MAGISTRI COSME CIVIS ROMANUS FUIT AMOTUM ALTARE.

(COSMATI) COSMAS AND SONS

ANAGNI: Duomo.

Pavement.

COSMAS CIVIS ROMANUS CUM FILIIS SUIS LUCA ET IACOBO HOC OPUS FECIT.

Venturi III, 791, note 1.

ANAGNI: Duomo.

Crypt S. Magnus.

Pavement.

+ MAGR COSMA CIVIS ROMANUS C̄Ū FILIIS SUIS LUCA ET IACOBO HOC OPUS FECIT.

SUBIACO: S. Scholastica.

Cloister.

COSMAS ET FILII LŪC ET ĪAC ĀLT ROMANI CIVES IN MARMORIS ARTE PERITI HOC OPUS EXPLERUNT ABĪS TP̄E LANDI.

(COSMATI) COSMATUS

[ROME: SS. Giovanni e Paolo.

Ciborium.

MAGISTER COSMATUS FECIT HOC OPUS MCCXXXV.]

ROME: Sancta Sanctorum Cappella.

Pilaster in Vestibule.

MAGISTER COSMATUS FECIT HOC OPUS.

(COSMATI) IOHANNES SON OF COSMATUS

ROME: S. Balbina.

Tomb of Stefano de Surdi.

ĪŌHS FILIUS MAGR̄I COSMATI FECIT HOC OPUS.

ROME: S. Maria Maggiore.

Tomb of Cardinal Rodriquez.

HOC ŌP FĒC IŌHES FILIUS MAGR̄I COSME CIVIS ROMANUS.

ROME: S. Maria sopra Minerva.

Tomb of Guglielmo Durand.

IŌHS FILIUS MAGR̄I COSMATI FĒC HOC ŌP.

(COSMATI) DRUDUS ET LUCAS

CIVITÀ CASTELLANA: Duomo.

Screen in Sacristy.

+ DRŪD' ET LUCAS CIVES ROMANI MAGR̄I DOCTISSIMI HOC OPUS FECERUNT.

(COSMATI) DEODATUS.

[ROME: S. Giacomo alla Lungara.
Pavement.

DEODATUS FILIUS COSMATI ET IACOBUS FECERUNT HOC OPUS.]

Crescimbeni, quoted Venturi III, p. 792, note.

ROME: S. Giovanni in Laterano.
A fragment.

HOC OPUS FECIT MAGISTER DEODATUS.

(Venturi III, p. 792, note.)

ROME: S. Maria in Cosmedin.
Ciborium.

DEODATUS ME FECIT.

Cappella Capizucchi.
Fragment.

HOC OPUS FECIT MAGRI DEODATUS.

TERAMO (ABRUZZI): Duomo.
Portal.

DIODATUS ROMANUS MCCXXXII.

TIVOLI: S. Pietro in Columna.
Fragment of Pavement.

MAGISTER DEODATUS FECIT HOC OPUS.

VASSALLETTUS

ANAGNI: Duomo.
Episcopal Throne.

VASALET DE ROMA ME FECIT. PRAESUL HONORANDUS HOC DAT NOMINE LANDUS.

ANAGNI: Duomo.
Candelabrum.

VASSALETO ME FECIT.

CIVITÀ LAVINIA (LANUVIO): Museo.
Fragment of Architrave.

. . . SSALLETTUS FECIT HOC OPUS ARCHIPRESBITERO IOHS.

Cf. C. Pinzi: *I principali monumenti di Viterbo* (Viterbo, 1894), p. 42.

[ROME: S. Apollinare.
Iconostasis fragment.

+ MAGISTER BASSALLETTUS ME FECIT.]

Cf. Venturi, *op. cit.,* III, p. 79, note.

ROME: SS. Apostoli.
Lion in portico.
BASSALECTUS.

[ROME: SS. Cosma e Damiano.
Tomb of Cardinal Guido.

. . . ROMANI BASILETTI INCIDIT (1154?).]

See G. Giovannoni in *L'Arte,* 1908, p. 279 and note.

[ROME: S. Croce in Gerusalemine.
Fragment.

. . . SALLECTUS ME FECIT.]

Cf. *Boll. dell'Ist. di Corr. archeol.,* 1830, p. 164 and G. Giavannoni,
L'Arte (1908), p. 281.

ROME: S. Giovanni in Laterano.
Cloister.

NOBILIT̄ DOCT̄ HAC VASSALLECTUS Ī ARTE C̄Ū PATRE CEPIT OPS Q̄D SŌL
PERFECIT IP̄E

ROME: S. Paolo fuori le mura.
Candelabrum.

EGO NICOLAUS DE ANGILO CUM PETRO BASSALECTO HOC OPUS C̄OPLEVI
(1170?)
Cloister.
MAGISTER PETRUS FECIT HOC OPUS.

[ROME: S. Pudenziana.
Portal.

+ MAGISTER VASSALLETTUS FECIT HOC OPUS.]

ROME: S. Saba.
Screen.

+ MAGISTER BASSALLETTUS ME FECIT QUI SIT BENEDICTUS.

[SEGNI : Duomo.

PETRUS BASSALETUS MCLXXXV.]

Cf. Lauri, *Storia,* quoted by Giovannoni, *op. cit.*

VITERBO: S. Francesco.
Tabernacle.

M. VASSALECTUS ME FECIT.

This is a work of the bottega.
Venturi calls the inscription ''scritta apocrifa''.

ANDREAS

ALBA FUCENSE (destroyed in the earthquake of 1915).
Iconostasis (fragments remain).

ANDREAS MAGISTER ROMANUS FECIT HOC OPUS.

See also Alba Fucense under RANUCIUS.

BINELLUS ET RODULFUS

BEVAGNA: S. Michele.
Portal.

RODULFUS + BINELLŪ FECER̄ EC OPERA X̄PS BENEDICAT ILO SENPER + MICHAEL CUSTODIAT.

DRUDUS DE TRIVIO

CIVITÀ CASTELLANA: Duomo.
Screen in Sacristy.

+ DRŪD' ET LUCAS CIVES ROMANI MAGR̄I DOCTISSIMI HOC OPUS FECERUNT.

FERENTINO: Duomo.
Ciborium.

+ MAGISTER DRUDUS DE TRIVIO CIVIS ROMANUS FECIT HOC OPUS.

ROME: S. Francesca Romana. On a stone in the angle of the first chapel on left.

DRUDUS DE TRIVIO H . . OP . . IS MAG . . . R FUIT.

ROME: Museo delle Terme.
In a Lavabo.

MAGR DRUDUS ME FECIT.

Cf. Giovannoni. *Op. cit.*

ODERICUS (?PETRUS ODERISI)

LONDON: Westminster Abbey.
Pavement of Sanctuary (1268).

+ XPI MILLENO BICENTENO DUODENO CUM SEXAGENO SUBDUCTUS QUATUOR ANNO TERTIUS HENRICUS REX URBS ODERICUS ET ABBAS HOS COMPEGERE PORPHYREOS LAPIDES.

PASCHALIS

ROME: S. Maria in Cosmedin.
Paschal Candelabrum.

VIR PB̄US ET DOCT PASCHALIS RITE VOCAT SŪMO CUM STUDIO CODĪDIT HOC CEREUM.

Cf. Promis, *Not. Epig.*, p. 28.

VITERBO: Museo Civico.

Sphinx.

HOC OPUS FECIT FR. PASCHALIS ROMANUS ORDINIS PD MCCLXXXVI.

PETRO DE MARIA

SASSOVIVO (near Foligno).

Cloister.

HOC CLAUSTRI OPUS EGREGIUM QUOD DECORAT MONASTERIUM DONNUS
ABBAS ANGELUS PERCEPIT MULTO SUMPTER FIERI ET FECIT A MAGISTRO
PETRO DE MARIA ROMANO OPERE ET MASTRIA ANNO DOMINI MILLENO
IUNCTO EI BIS CENTENO NONO QUOQUE CUM VICENO.

PETRUS ODERISI

VITERBO: S. Francesco.

Tomb of Clement IV. (d. 1268).

PETRUS ODERISI SEPULCRI FECIT HOC OPUS.

(Papebroch: Conatus chron. historicus ad catalogum Romanorum
Pontificum.)

PETRUS ROMANUS (?PETRUS ODERISI)

LONDON: Westminster Abbey.

Shrine of S. Edward Confessor, 1269 (?).

(1) + ANNO MILENO DOMINI CUM SEXAGENO ET

(2) BIS CENTENO CUM COMPLETO QUASI DENO HOC OPUS EST FACTUM
QUOD PETRUS

(3) DUXIT IN ACTUM ROMANUS CIVIS HOMO

(4) CAUSAM NOSCERE SI VIS REX FUIT HENRICUS SANCTI PRESENTIS AMICUS.
(Reading of Widmore and Neale.)

RAINALDUS

FARFA: Badia.

Fragment in Pavement, possibly part of iconostasis or ambo.

RAINALDUS.

INDEX OF PLACES

ROME

S. ALESSIO IN AVENTINO.
>Two columns from the Iconostasis of S. Bartolommeo all'Isola, one signed:
>
>IACOBUS LAURENTII FECIT HAS DECEM ET NOVEM COLUMPNAS CUM CAPITELLIS SUIS

S. ANTONIO ABATE.
>Portal (1269) with two sphinxes.
>The inscription over the door refers to Cardinal Capocci, patron of the hospital.

SS. APOSTOLI.
>Lion of Portal signed:
>
>BASSALECTUS.

S. BALBINA.
>Bishop's Throne.
>Tomb of Cardinal Stefano dei Surdi, signed:
>
>IŌHS FILIUS MAGRI COSMATI FECIT HOC OPUS.
>
>The arms of the Cardinal in mosaic, white on blue ground.

S. BARTOLOMMEO ALL'ISOLA.
>Portico (1113).

S. CECILIA IN TRASTEVERE.
>Portico.
>Paschal Candelabrum (? by Arnolfo).

S. CESAREO.
>Two Ambones (that on left far the finer).
>Screens.
>High Altar.
>Two Side Altars.
>Bishop's Throne.
>Base of Paschal Candelabrum.
>Ciborio?
>
>The ciborio is of the XIIth cent. according to Venturi (III, p. 886) but seems to be part of the restoration of Clement VIII.

S. CLEMENTE.
    Pavement.
    Ciborium.
    Tabernacle for Eucharist (1299).
    Ambone.
    Screens.

S. COSIMATO.
    Cloister.

S. CRISOGONO.
    Cloister.
    Pavement.

S. CROCE IN GERUSALEMME.
    Pavement panels in nave.

S. GIORGIO IN VELABRO.
    Portico.
    Campanile.
    Pavement.
    Ciborium.

SS. GIOVANNI E PAOLO.
    Portico.
    Campanile.
    Pavement (relaid 1911).
    Altar.

S. GIOVANNI IN LATERANO.
    Pavement panels in nave
    Kneeling figure of Pope.
    Cloister signed:

      + NOBILIT̄. DOCT̄ HAC VASSALLECTUS Ī ARTE C̄V PATRE CEPIT OPS, Q̄D SŌL
        PERFECIT IP̄E.

    Bishop's Throne in Cloister.
    Various fragments in Cloister.

S. GIOVANNI A PORTA LATINA.
    Portal.
    Altar mosaics.

S. GREGORIO MAGNO.
    Pavement (remade in XVIIIth century).

S. LORENZO FUORI LE MURA.

Portico.
Pavement.
Ciborium signed:

IOHS PETRUS ANGELUS ET SASSO FILII PAULI MARMORARII HUIUS OP MAGISTRI
FUERUNT MCXLVIII.

Pulpit.
Screen.
Bishop's Throne.
Tomb of Cardinal Fieschi.
Cloister.

S. LORENZO IN LUCINA.

Campanile.
Portico.
Altar frontal.
Bishop's Throne inscribed:

TEMPORE DOMINI PASCALIS II PAPA ANNO EIUS XIII MILLESIMO CENTESIMO XII
INDICTIONE V. VI KALENDAS FEBRUARI P MANUS EIUSDEM PONTIFILIS . . .

The inscription establishes the presence in the altar of the relics of the Grati-
cola—the fishing net—and of two *ampulle* of the blood of S. Lorenzo. The
throne is composed of marble of the Imperial epoch.

S. MARCO.

Ciborium signed:

IOHS PETRUS ANGELUS SASSO FILII PAULI HUIUS OPERIS MAGISTRI FUERUNT.

Pavement (relaid).

S. MARIA IN ARACOELI.

Pavement.
Two pulpits or Ambones. That on right is signed:

LAURENTIUS CUM IACOBO FILIO SUO HUIUS OPERIS MAGISTER FUIT.

Tomb of Honorius IV.
Tomb of Luca Savelli.
Tomb of Cardinal Acquasparta (1304).
Subterranean altar called of Augustus inscribed:

LUMINIS HANC ALMAM MATRIS QUI SCANDIS AD AULAM CUNTARUM PRIMA QUE
FUIT ORBE SITA.

NOSCAS QUOD CESAR TUNC STRUXIT OCTAVIANUS HANC ARA CELI SACRA PROLES
CUM PATET EI.

S. MARIA IN COSMEDIN.
> Campanile.
> Portico.
> Pavement inscribed:
> ALFANUS FIERI TIBI FECIT VIRGO MARIA.
> Ambone.
> Paschal Candelabrum inscribed:
> VIR PBUS ET DOCTUS PASCHALIS RITE VOCAT SUMO CUM STUDIO CODIDIT HOC
> > CEREUM.
> Ciborium signed:
> DEODATUS ME FECIT.
> Church reconstructed 1894-99.
> The Ciborio was by Deodatus, son of Cosmas II: the rest by Paulus.

S. MARIA MAGGIORE.
> Pavement (all reconstructed temp. Benedict XIV).
> Tomb of Consalvo Rodriquez signed:
> HOC OP FEC IOHES FILIUS MAGRI COSME CIVIS ROMANUS.
> Paliotto.

S. MARIA SOPRA MINERVA.
> Tomb of Durante di Mende signed:
> IOHS FILIUS MAGRI COSMATI FEC HOC OP.

S. MARIA IN NAVICELLA.
> Pavement: date (?).

S. MARIA IN TRASTEVERE.
> Pavement.

SS. NEREO ED ACHILLEO.
> Ciborium.
> Altar.
> Screen.
> Bishop's Throne on Lions.
> Pavement.
> Two Ambones (one from S. Silvestro in Capite).
> Paschal Candelabrum—base only.

S. PAOLO FUORI LE MURA.
> Paschal Candelabrum signed:
> EGO NICOLAUS DE ANGILO CUM PETRO BASSALECTO HOC OPUS COPLEVI.

Cloister inscribed:

HOC OPUS ARTE SUA QUEM ROMA CARDO BEAVIT/NATUS DE CAPUA PETRUS OLIM
PRIMITAVIT ARDEA QUEM GENUIT QUIBUS ABBAS VIXIT IN ANNIS/CETERA
DISPOSUIT BENE PROVIDA DEXTRA IOHANNIS.

Begun by Abbot Peter II of Capua (1193-1208), completed by Abbot John V
(1208-1241). The latest side is signed:

MAGISTER PETRUS FECIT HOC OPUS.

S. PIETRO IN VATICANO.
Cappella della Pietà: Spiral Column.
Eight spiral columns in the galleries under the dome.
Two spiral columns in the altar on right in the Cappella del Ss. Sacramento.
See also under Trinità de' Monti.
On these and other similar columns in the Trinità de' Monti in Rome, in S.
Carlo at Cave and in S. Chiara in Naples, see E. Mauceri: *Colonne tortili così
dette del Tempio di Salamone* in *L'Arte* (1898), pp. 377 *et seq.*

GROTTE VATICANE
Episcopal Throne.

S. PRASSEDE.
Pavement.
Tomb of Cardinal Ancherus of Troyes.
In crypt: Paliotto in mosaic.

S. PUDENZIANA.
Campanile.
Portal (restored).

SS. QUATTRO CORONATI.
Cloister.
Pavement.

S. SABA.
Portico and façade signed:

+ HOC OPUS DNO IOHANNE ABBATE BENE FACTUM EST P. MANUS MAGISTRI
IACOBI +

Pavement.
Screen, signed:

+ MAGISTER BASSALLETTUS ME FECIT QUI SIT BENEDICTUS.
Bishop's Throne.

S. SABINA.

Cloister: Arches decorated with Cosmatesque mosaic.
Schola cantorum, reconstructed.
Bishop's Throne.
Tombstones.

SANCTA SANCTORUM CAPPELLA.

Pavement.
Decoration. On a pillar to left of entry is the signature:

MAGISTER COSMATUS FECIT HOC OPUS.

S. TOMMASO IN FORMIS.

Portal signed:

MAGISTER IACOBUS CUM FILIO SUO COSMATO FECIT HOC OPUS.

SS. TRINITÀ DE' MONTI.

Two spiral columns.
(See under S. Pietro in Vaticano.)

OUTSIDE ROME

ALBA FUCENSE (ABRUZZI)
S. Pietro.

> The Cosmatesque decoration and furniture were destroyed in the earth-
> quake of 1915. The Ambone and some other remains are preserved in
> a small building before the ruined church.

> The Ambone is signed:

CIVIS ROMAN DOCTISSIMUS ARTE I͞O͞HS CUI COLLEGA BONUS ANDREAS
DETULIT HONUS HOC OPUS EXCELSUM STRUSSERUNT MENTE PERITI
NOBILIS ET PRUDENS ODERISIUS ABFUIT ABAS.

> Cf. Promis : *Op. cit.* p. 12 who reads DELUIT.
> The Iconostasis was signed by Andreas alone:

ANDREAS MAGISTER ROMANUS FECIT HOC OPUS.

ALBANO
Frattocchie.

> Just beyond the inn is a church with pieces of Cosmati mosaic.

S. Pietro.

> Campanile.

AMASENO
S. Lorenzo.

> Portal.

ANAGNI
Duomo: S. Maria.

> Pavement (ca. 1226, relaid 1882), signed:

MAGIST COSMAS HOC OP FECIT.

> (This inscription is now in the museum with another, see below.)

> Paschal Candelabrum signed:

VASSALETO ME FECIT (restored 1904).

> Episcopal Throne, signed:

VASALE͞T DE ROMA ME FECIT and inscribed PRÆSUL HONORANDUS HOC
DAT NOMINE LANDUS.

> Ciborium.
> Tomb of the Caetani family (Third Chapel L.) (after 1294)

CRYPT: S. MAGNUS.
Pavement signed (1231):

MA G̅R̅. COSMAS CIVIS ROMANUS C̅V̅ FILIIS SUIS LUCA ET IACOBO HOC OPUS
FECIT.

MUSEUM.
Collection of Cosmatesque fragments and inscriptions, among them:

ANNO DOMINI MCCXXXI PER MANUS MAGISTRI COSME CIVIS ROMANUS FUIT
AMOTUM ALTARE.

This was the altar of S. Magnus in the crypt moved to complete the
pavement there.

ÁRSOLI
CASTELLO MASSIMO.
Cappella façade, Cosmatesque decoration.

ASSISI
S. FRANCESCO, LOWER CHURCH.
Pulpit.
High Altar (restored).
Tomb of "Queen of Cyprus."
Tomb behind the Blessed Sacrament altar.
Walls of altar recess of Madgalen Chapel.

S. FRANCESCO, UPPER CHURCH.
Rose window.
Altar (entirely remade).
Bishop's Throne (restored).
Decoration.

BEVAGNA
S. MICHELE.
Portal signed:

RODULFUS + BINELLŪ FECE̅R̅ EC OPERA X̅P̅S̅ BENEDICAT ILO SENPER
+ MICHAEL CUSTODIAT.

(Binellus also signed the portal of the XIIth cent. church, S. Silvestro,
dated 1197 hard by S. Michele and very well preserved. Cf. also the
frieze about the door of S. Maria Maggiore in Spello and the doors of
the Duomo, S. Pietro and S. Salvatore in Spoleto which all seem to be
related to the work of Binellus at Bevagna. Only in the two churches
of Bevagna did he or he and Rodulfus sign.)

CANTERBURY
CATHEDRAL.
Pavement in St. Thomas's Chapel.

CASTEL S. ELIA (near NEPI).
>   Ciborium (XIth cent.).
>   Pavement, only very rough fragments, except in Sanctuary where relaid.

CAVA DEI TIRRENI
>   Badia della SS. Trinità.
>>   Ambone.
>>   Paschal candelabrum.

CAVE
>   S. Carlo.
>>   Two spiral columns.
>>>   (See under Rome: S. Pietro in Vaticano.)

CIVITÀ CASTELLANA
>   Duomo.
>>   Façade with Rose, central Portal with Lions. Right side—Door with mosaic.
>>   The Central Portal is signed:

> LAURENTIUS CUM IACOBO FILIO SUO MAGISTRI DOCTISSIMI ROMANI H̄ OPUS FECERUNT.

>>   The Side Door is signed:

> M̄A IACO + RAINERIUS PETRI RODULFI FIERI FECIT + BUS M. FECIT.

>>   Portico with Triumphal Arch is signed:

> MAGISTER IACOBUS CIVIS ROMANUS CUM COSMA FILIO SUO CARISSIMO FECIT HOC OPUS ANNO DNI MCCX.

>>   A fragment of inscription on left of Triumphal Arch reads [IACO] BUS LA [URE]NTII
>>   Pavement in Nave and Presbytery.
>>   Crypt.
>>   Choir stalls in Sacristy.
>>>   On Epistle side Lion and Lioness at base, signed :

> DRUD' ET LUCAS CIVES ROMANI MAGR̄I DOCTISSIMI HOC OPUS FECERUNT.

>>>   On Gospel side Lion and Sphinx at base.
>>   In the garden is a marble arch with mosaic from the Iconostasis.

CORI
>   S. Maria della Pietà.
>>   Paschal Candelabrum (? earliest known).

FALLERI
>   S. Maria di Falleri (near Civitá Castellana).
>>   Portal signed:

> LAURENTIUS CUM IACOBO FILIO SUO FECIT HOC OPUS.

>>   There was a cross in mosaic over the door but that has perished.
>>   Rose in apse.

FARFA IN SABINA

Badia.

Pavement.

Parts of the Ambone now in pavement signed: RAINALDUS.

FERENTINO

Duomo.

Pavement.

Altar.

Screen before altar signed:

HOC OPIFEX MAGNUS FECIT VIR NOMINE PAULUS . . . PRESUL ERAT SUMMUS PASCHALIS PAPA SECUNDUS (1100-1118).

Ciborium signed:

MAGISTER DRUDUS DE TRIVIO CIVIS ROMANUS FECIT HOC OPUS. Given by the Archdeacon of Norwich, a native of Ferentino.

Paschal Candelabrum.

Bishop's Throne.

Sacristy Door: Sphinx and Lion.

PALAZZO EPISCOPALE—Carcere di S. Ambrogio—Ciborio.

FLORENCE

Opera del Duomo.

Sala della antica facciata del Duomo.

Fragment from old façade of the Cathedral where it formed the lunette above the central door behind the marble group of the Madonna and Child by Arnolfo di Cambio.

Above this group is displayed in the Opera a part of the Cosmatesque architrave from the façade.

Sala Terza: Paschal Candelabrum XIIIth century (small).

FOLIGNO

Duomo.

Lateral Portal.

(Said to have been brought by sea, but apparently by RODULFUS and BINELLUS OF BEVAGNA.)

Environs: BADIA DI SASSOVIVO.

Cloister by Pietro de Maria 1229. (See under Sassovivo.)

FONDI

Duomo.

Ambone signed:

TABULA . MARMOREA . VITREIS . DISTINCTA . LAPILLIS . DOCTORIS . STUDIO . SIC . EST . ERECTA . IOHANNIS . ROMANO . GENITI COGNOMINE NICOLAO. (?Nicolaus de Angelo.)

Bishop's Throne.

FORONOVO

S. Maria in Vescovio.

Cardinal Gaetano Lai in or about 1932 in restoring the church did away with what remained of the Cosmati pavement. Nothing now remains attributable to the "Cosmati".

FOSSANOVA

Badia.

Cosmatesque Portal.

GAETA

Duomo.

Paschal Candelabrum.

Two fragments of Ambone almost certainly Campanian, similar to the Pulpits at Sessa Aurunca, Ravello, Amalfi, Salerno, Benevento.

The Jonah in mosaic or sculpture is characteristic of the Campanian school.

GENAZZANO

S. Nicola.

Pavement.

GROTTAFERRATA

Badia.

Fragments of monuments of the Counts of Tusculum, remains of an altar, mosaic work etc.

Pavement.

LONDON

Westminster Abbey.

Pavement in Sanctuary signed:

+ XPI MILLENO BICENTENO DUODENO CUM SEXAGENO SUBDUCTUS QUATUOR ANNO TERTIUS HENRICUS REX URBS ODERICUS ET ABBAS HOS COMPEGERE PORPHYREOS LAPIDES.

Chapel of S. Edward Confessor.

Shrine signed:

+ ANNO MILENO DOMINI CUM SEXAGENO ET BIS CENTENO CUM COMPLETO QUASI DENO HOC OPUS EST FACTUM QUOD PETRUS DUXIT IN ACTUM ROMANUS CIVIS HOMO CAUSAM NOSCERE SI VIS REX FUIT HENRICUS SANCTI PRESENTIS AMICUS.

(Widmore: *Hist. of Church of S. Peter, Westminster* (1751), and Neale (1818). Lethaby: *Westminster Abbey* (1906), prefers the reading SEPTUAGENO for SEXAGENO.)

Pavement.

Tomb of Henry III.

Tomb of Princes, John, Alfonso and Katherine, removed to ambulatory.

Grave stones of John and Margaret de Valence.

LUCCA
    S. Frediano.
        Pavement. Some remains in choir.

LUGNANO IN TEVERINA (near Orvieto)
    S. Maria Assunta.
        Portico with rose and reliefs and mosaic work.
        Pavement (fragments remain).
        Crypt.

MONTEBUONO
    S. Pietro.
        Campanile.

NAPLES
    S. Chiara.
        Two spiral columns perhaps from Castel del Monte. (See under S. Pietro
           in Vaticano.)

NARNI
    Duomo.
        Pavement fragments.
    S. Maria in Penzola: Shrine of SS. Giovenale and Cassio.
    S. Domenico: Pavement fragments.

NAZZANO
    Badia di S. Antimo (restored by Government in 1918).
        Pavement much ruined but still beautiful.
        Schola Cantorum.
        Ambone on Gospel side.

NEPI
    Duomo.
        A small fragment of Cosmati mosaic has been placed in wall under portico,
           possibly part of original pavement of nave.
        Crypt.

NINFA
    Church Outside Walls.
        Campanile and apse with Cosmatesque decoration.

ORTE
    S. Silvestro.
        Campanile.

ORVIETO
    S. Andrea.
        Portal.
        Pavement much ruined.
        Pulpit.

S. Bartolomenco.
>   Portal.
Near Orvieto: Badia SS. Severo e Martirio. (3 kil. outside Porta Romana)
>   Pavement.
>   Campanile (12 sided).

PALESTRINA
Duomo.
>   Paliotto formed of fragments of the Cosmati pavement.

PALOMBARA SABINA (near)
S. Giovanni in Argentella.
>   Early Ciborium.
>   Iconostasis inscribed.

>   . . . anno centeno septuagesimo atque milleno (1170).

>   Outside, one of the steps is part of a Cosmatesque architrave.
>   Campanile.

PISA
Duomo.
>   Pavement, large fragment.
>   Outside, the Cathedral is decorated in places with what is apparently
>   Cosmatesque mosaic.
Baptistery—Pavement—fragment relaid.
Campo Santo—fragment of mosaic.

PONZANO ROMANO
S. Andrea in Flumine.
>   Ciborium signed:

>   + nicolaus cum suis filiis iohn et gvittone fecerunt hoc opus.

>   Pavement.
>   Screen.
>   Altar and shrine under.
>   Ambone (was signed and dated 1209).

RIGNANO FLAMINO
SS. Abbondio ed Abbondanzio.
>   Campanile.

ROCCA DI BOTTE (Abruzzi)
Badia.
>   Ciborio.
>   Ambone.

SASSOVIVO
>BADIA (near Foligno).
>>Cloister with this inscription:

>>HOC CLAUSTRI OPUS EGREGIUM QUOD DECORAT MONASTERIUM DONNUS ABBAS ANGELUS PERCEPIT MULTO SUMPTER FIERI ET FECIT A MAGISTRO PETRO DE MARIA ROMANO OPERE ET MASTRIA ANNO DOMINI MILLENO IUNCTO ET BIS CENTENO HONO QUORUE CUM VICENO.

SEGNI
>DUOMO.
>>Chapel of S. Bruno; part of Iconostasis now altar.

S. PIETRO
>>Paliotto.
>>Campanile.

SPOLETO
>DUOMO.
>>Pavement.

SUBIACO
>S. SCHOLASTICA.
>>Cloisters signed over the archivault of doorway on south side.

>>+ MAGISTER IACOBUS ROMAN FECIT HOC OP;

>>and again on architrave:

>>>COSMAS ET FILII LUC ET IAC ALT. ROMANI CIVES IN MARMORIS ARTE PERITI HOC OPUS EXPLERUNT ABIS TPE LANDI.

>Sacro Speco.
>>Abbot's Throne.
>>Pavement of Upper Church.
>>Altar.
>>Portal signed:

>>+ SIT PAX INTRANTI SIT GRATIA DIGNA PRECANTI + LAURENTIUS CUM IACOBO FILIO SUO FECIT HOC OPUS.

SUTRI
>DUOMO.
>>Campanile.
>>Main Portal.
>>Pavement restored.
>>Crypt.

>S. GIACOMO—Pavement (only a small fragment).

>S. FRANCESCO—Altar (Venturi *St. dell' Arte Ital. III*, p. 778).

TARQUINIA (Corneto)

S. Maria di Castello.

Portal signed:

PETRUS RANUCII (1143). (See under Ranucius.)

Window signed:

NICOLAUS RANUCII MAGISTER ROMANUS FECIT.

Pavement.

Ciborio signed:

IOHANNES ET GUITTO MAGISTRI HOC OPUS FECERUNT MCLXVI—(much modernised).

Ambone signed:

HOC OP NITIDUM AURO ET MARMORE DIVERSO FIERI FECIT . . . PER MANUS MAGISTRI IOHS GUITTONIS CIVIS RMN.

TERAMO (Abruzzi)

Duomo.

Portal with Triumphal arch, Rose and three niches with statues signed:

DIODATUS ROMANUS (1332).

In cortile beyond Sacristy a Tabernacle with four twisted columns standing on lions.

S. Francesco (S. Antonio).

Portal: three windows on left.

At back of church: window with twisted columns.

TERRACINA

Duomo.

Pavement (remains of).

Paschal Candelabrum.

Pulpit.

Vestibule mosaic freize.

TIVOLI

Duomo.

Fragments of Pavement.

Campanile.

S. Michele.

Campanile.

S. Maria Maggiore.

Fragments of Pavement.

Altar in R. aisle.

Two twisted columns.

S. Silvestro.

Fragments of Pavement.

S. Pietro.
Fragments of Pavement.

S. Andrea.
Fragments.

TOFFIA
S. Lorenzo.
Fragments in façade.

TUSCANIA (Toscanella)
S. Pietro.
Façade: Portal, Gallery and Rose.

VELLETRI
Duomo.
Over high altar a Reliquary in form of a Tempietto in Cosmati style.

VEROLI
S. Erasmo.
Portico.
Campanile.

VETRALLA
S. Francesco.
Pavement (much restored).

VITERBO
Duomo.
Pavement.

S. Francesco.
Rose window.
Pavement.
Tomb of Clement IV signed:

PETRUS ODERISI SEPULCRI FECIT HOC OPUS.

Tomb of Hadrian V (?Arnolfo).
Tomb of Di Vico.
Ciborietto signed:

M. VASSALECTUS ME FECIT (probably a forgery).

Museo Civico.   Sphinx signed:

HOC OPUS FECIT FR. PASCHALIS ROMANUS ORDINIS PD. A.D. MCCLXXXVI.

VULTURELLA IN SABINA
S. Maria in Vulturella.
Ciborio.
Pavement — a fragment before the altar.
Twisted column once perhaps the Paschal Candelabrum.

BIBLIOGRAPHY

AGAZZI (A.), *Il musaico in Italia* (Milano, 1926).

BOITO (C.), *Architettura Cosmatesca* (Milano, 1860).

BOITO (C.), *L'architettura del medioevo in Italia : I Cosmati* (Milano, 1880).

CECCHETTI (C.), *S. Clemente* (Roma, 1930).

CLAUSE (G.), *Les marbriers romains et le mobilier presbyteral* (Paris, 1897).

CLAUSE (G.), *Les Cosmati et l'Eglise de Cività Castellana* in *Revue de l'art Chretien* 1897), p. 271 et seq.

COLOSANTI (A.), *L'Aniene* (Bergamo, 1906).

COLOSANTI (A.), *S. Maria in Aracoeli* (*Le Chiese di Roma*) (Roma, 1923).

DASTI (L.) *Notizie storiche archeologiche di Tarquinia o Corneto* (Roma, 1878).

EROLI (G.), *Lugnano Teverina* (Narni, 1903).

EROLI (G.), *Descrizione delle Chiese di Narni* (? Narni, 1905).

FALOCI-PULIGNANI (M.), *Foligno* (Bergamo, 1907).

FALOCI-PULIGNANI (M.), *I marmorari romani a Sassovivo* (Perugia, 1915).
　Cf. *Archivio per la storia Eccles. dell'Umbria*, 1915, pp. 561 *et seq.*

FEDELE (P.), *L'iscrizione del Chiostro di S. Paolo* in *Archivio della Soc. romana di Storia patria* (Roma, 1921), xliv, pp. 269-276.
　　Establishes that the Cloister of S. Paolo fuori le mura was finished before 1235.

FREY (C.), *Genealogie der Cosmati* in *Jahrb. der K. Preuss.* (1885).

FROTHINGHAM (A.), *Notes on roman artists of the middle age,* in *American Journal of Archeology,* 1890 (Boston, 1890), pp. 182, 307 *et seq.* 350.

FROTHINGHAM (A.), *Scoperta dell'epoca precisa della costruzione del chiostro Lateranense* in *Bullettino d'Archaeologia cristiana,* 1892 (Roma, 1892), p. 145 *et seq.*

FROTHINGHAM (A.), *The Monuments of Christian Rome* (New York, 1908).

GALASSI (G.), *Roma o Bisanzio* (Rome, 1930).

GENTILI (E.), *San Pietro in Toscanella* in *Archivio storico dell'Arte,* 1889, p. 361 *et seq.*

GIOVANNONI (G.), *I monasteri di Subiaco* (Roma, 1904), vol. i, pp. 313 *et seq.*

GIOVANNONI (G.), *Note sui marmorari romani* in *Arch. Soc. Rom. di Storia Pat.* (1904), p. 5 *et seq.*

GIOVANNONI (G.), *Opere dei Vassalletti,* in *L'Arte* (1908), p. 262 *et seq.*

GRISAR (H.), *Die rom Kapelle Sancta Sanctorum u. ihr Schatz* (Freiburg, 1908).

HUETTER (L.) and LAVAGNINO (E.), *S. Lorenzo in Lucina* (Roma, 1931).

HUTTON (E.), *An Unknown Victorian,* in *The Nineteenth Century and After* (London, January, 1934).

HUTTON (E.), *The New Pavement in the Sanctuary of Buckfast Abbey,* in *Buckfast Abbey Chronicle,* vol. xiii (1943), pp. 107-113.

LAVAGNINO (E.), *S. Paolo sulla via Ostiense* (Roma, 1924).

LAVAGNINO (E.) and MOSCHINI (V.), *S. Maria Maggiore* (Roma, 1923).

LETHABY (W. R.), *Westminster Abbey and the King's Craftsmen* (London, 1906).

LETHABY (W. R.), *Westminster Abbey Re-examined* (London, 1925).

LUGANO (P.), *L. Abbazia di S. Croce di Sassovivo* (Roma, 1912).

MADONI (E.), *Pavimento del battistero fiorentino* (Brescia, 1914).
  (On the Cosmatesque pavements in the Duomo at Pisa and S. Frediano at Lucca.)

MAUCERI (E.), *Colonne Tortili* in *L'Arte,* 1898, pp. 377 *et seq.*

MUÑOZ (A.), *S. Pietro in Vaticano* (Roma, 1923).

ORTOLANI (S.), *S. Croce in Gerusalemme* (Roma, n.d.).

ORTOLANI (S.), *S. Giovanni in Laterano* (Roma, 1925).

ORTOLANI (S.), *SS. Giovanni e Paolo* (Roma, n.d.).

PROMIS (C.), *Notizie epigrafiche degli artefici marmorari romani dal X al XV sec.* (Turin, 1836).

ROSSI (G. B. DE), *Del così detto opus alexandrinum e dei marmorarii romani in S. Maria di Castello, Tarquinia,* in *Bullettino di Archæologia Cristiana,* 1875 (Roma, 1875), pp. 110 *et seq.*

ROSSI (G. B. DE), *Tabernacolo altare e sua capsella reliquaria in S. Stefano presso Fiano Romano* in *Bull. di Achæologia Cristiana,* 1888-9 (Roma, 1889), pp. 154 *et seq.*

ROSSI (G. B. DE), *Raccolta di iscrizioni romane relative ad artisti ed alle loro opere nel medioevo* in *Bull. di Archæologia Cristiana,* 1891 (Roma, 1891), pp. 73-101.

ROSSI (G. B. DE), *Musaici cristiani e saggi dei pavimenti delle chiese di Roma anteriori al secolo XV* (Roma, 1899).

SALAZARO (D.), *L'arte romano nel medioevo :* appendice di *Monumenti dell'Italia mediovale,* III (Naples, 1881).

SANTILI (A.), *La Basilica SS. Apostoli* (Roma, 1925).

SIBILIA (S.), *Guida storico-artistica della Cattedrale di Anagni* (Anagni, 1936).

SPINELLI (R.), *S. Maria sopra Minerva* (Roma, 1925).

STEVENSON (E. Henry), in *Conferenza della Soc. cultori della cristiana archeologia* in *Bullettino d'Archeologia cristiana,* 1880 (Roma, 1880), pp. 59 *et seq.*
  See also vols for 1871, 1875, 1878 and 1882.

STEVENSON (E. Henry), *Mostra della città di Roma all'Esposizione di Torino del 1884* (Roma, 1884).

TAGGI (C.), *Della fabbrica della Cattedrale di Anagni* (Roma, 1888).

TAURISANO (P. I., O.P.), *S. Sabina* (Roma, n.d.).

TESORO DELLA CAPPELLA SANCTA SANCTORUM, *Biblioteca Apost. Vaticana Museo Sacro—Guida LV* (Città del Vaticano, 1941).

THYNNE (R.), *The Churches of Rome* (London, 1924).

TOESCA (P.), *Storia dell'Arte Italiana* (Milano, 1927), Vol. 2, pp. 582 *et seq.* 667, note 826 *et seq.*

TOMASSETTI (G.), *Dei Sodalizi in genere e dei marmorari romani* in *Bull. della Comm. Arch. Comunale* (Roma, 1906).

URBINI (G.), *Spello, Bevagna, Montefalco* (Bergamo, 1913).

VENTURI (A.), *Storia dell'Arte italiana,* vol. III, pp. 771 *et seq.* (Milano, 1904).

ZAMBARELLI (P. L., C.R.S.), *SS. Bonifacio ed Alessio* (Roma, N.D.).

PLATES

1. CAMPANILE

Rome: SS. Giovanni e Paolo

2B.   CAMPANILE AND PORCH

Rome: S. Maria in Cosmedin

2A.   CAMPANILE

Rome: S. Pudenziana

3. CAMPANILE AND PORTICO

Rome: S. Giorgio in Velabro

4A. CLOISTER

Rome: S. Cosimato (*circa* 1200)

4B. CLOISTER

Rome: SS. Quattro Coronati. Paulus (?) (*circa* 1113)

5A. CLOISTER

Rome: S. Paolo fuori le Mura. Vassallettus

5B. CLOISTER

Subiaco: S. Scholastica. Jacobus Cosmatus and his sons

6A. CLOISTER

Rome : S. Giovanni in Laterano. Vassallettus

6B. CLOISTER

Rome : S. Giovanni in Laterano. Vassallettus

7A. CLOISTER: DETAIL

Rome: S. Giovanni in Laterano. Vassallettus

7B. SPHINX

Rome: S. Giovanni in Laterano Cloister. Vassallettus

8. CLOISTER

9B.   CLOISTER: DETAIL

Rome: S. Paolo fuori le Mura.   Vassallettus

9A.   CLOISTER: DETAIL

Subiaco: S. Scholastica.   Jacobus Cosmatus

10B.   PORTAL

Tarquinia : S. Maria in Castello. Petrus Ranucii (portal) and
Nicolaus Ranucii (window)

10A.   CLOISTER: DETAIL

Sassovivo, near Foligno. Abbazia di S. Croce
Petrus de Maria

11.　INTERIOR AND PAVEMENT

Rome: S. Clemente

12. FAÇADE

13B. ROSE

Tuscania : S. Pietro

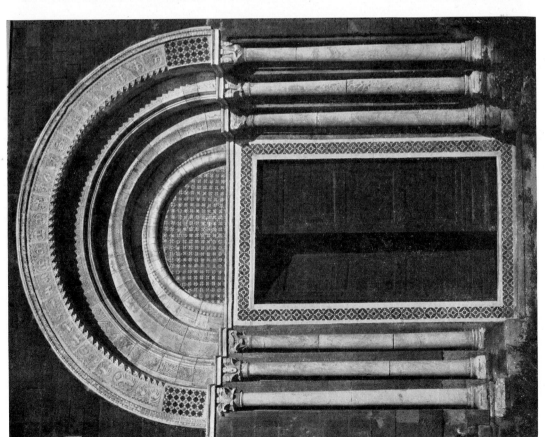

13A. PORTAL

Tuscania : S. Pietro

14. PORTICO, CAMPANILE AND FAÇADE

Rome: S. Lorenzo fuori le Mura. Paulus (?)

15B. PORTAL

Rome : S. Tommaso in Formis. Jacobus and his son Cosmas

15A. SIDE PORTAL

Cività Castellana : Duomo. Jacobus Cosmatus

16. PORTICO AND FAÇADE

Cività Castellana: Duomo. Laurentius Cosmatus and his son Jacobus and grandson Cosmas

17. TRIUMPHAL ARCH AND ROSE

Città Castellana: Duomo. Jacobus Cosmatus and his son Cosmas

18. CENTRAL PORTAL

Cività Castellana: Duomo. Laurentius Cosmatus and his son Jacobus

19. CIBORIUM AND ALTAR

Castel S. Elia: S. Elia

20. CIBORIUM, ALTAR AND CONFESSION

Rome: S. Giorgio in Velabro

21. CIBORIUM, SCREEN AND CONFESSION

Anagni: Duomo. Vassallettus

22. CIBORIUM, ALTAR, CONFESSION AND SCREEN

Ponzano: S. Andrea in Flumine. Nicolaus Ranucii and his sons Johannes and Guitto

23. CIBORIUM, ALTAR, CONFESSION AND SCREEN

Ferentino: Duomo. Drudus de Trivio

24A.   ALTAR FRONT

Rome: S. Prassede

24B.   ALTAR OF THE SACRED MANGER

Rome: S. Maria Maggiore

25. ALTAR

Subiaco : Sacro Speco

26. EPISCOPAL THRONE AND SCREEN

Rome: S. Lorenzo fuori le Mura

27. EPISCOPAL THRONE

Anagni: Duomo. Vassallettus

28B. EPISCOPAL THRONE

Rome: SS. Nereo ed Achilleo

28A. EPISCOPAL THRONE

Rome: S. Sabina

29B. EPISCOPAL THRONE
Assisi : S. Francesco

29A. EPISCOPAL THRONE
Rome : S. Cesareo

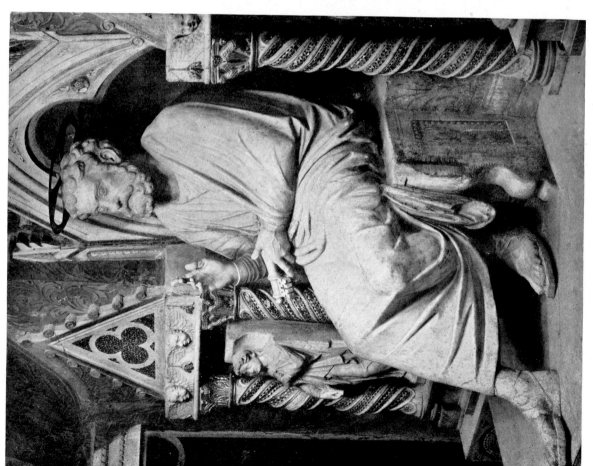

31. AMBONE (XII CENT.) AND PASCHAL CANDELABRUM

Rome: S. Clemente

32. AMBONE AND PASCHAL CANDELABRUM (XIII CENT.)

Rome : S. Lorenzo fuori le Mura

33. AMBONE (XII CENT.) AND PASCHAL CANDELABRUM

Rome: S. Maria in Cosmedin

34B. AMBONE

Rome : S. Maria in Aracoeli. Laurentius Cosmatus and his son Jacobus

34A. AMBONE

Rome : S. Maria in Aracoeli. Laurentius Cosmatus and his son Jacobus

35. AMBONE

Tarquinia: S. Maria in Castello. Johannes Ranucius

36. PULPIT

Orvieto: S. Andrea

37. AMBONE

Rome: S. Cesareo

38. PULPIT

Fondi: S. Pietro. Johannes son of Nicolaus Romanus

39. PASCHAL CANDELABRUM

Rome: S. Paolo fuori le Mura

Nicolaus de Angilo and Petrus Vassallettus

40A & B. DETAILS OF PASCHAL CANDELABRUM

Rome: S. Paolo fuori le Mura

41. DETAIL OF PASCHAL CANDELABRUM
Rome: S. Paolo fuori le Mura

42A. PASCHAL CANDELABRUM

Cori: Duomo

42B. PASCHAL CANDELABRUM

Ferentino: Duomo

43A & B. PASCHAL CANDELABRUM

Anagni : Duomo. Vassallettus

44A & B. PASCHAL CANDELABRUM

Terracina: Duomo

45A. PANEL FROM DISMANTLED SCREEN

Ferentino : Duomo

45B. PANELS FROM DISMANTLED SCREENS

Anagni : Duomo

46. CHOIR SCREEN

Rome : S. Cesareo

47. CHOIR SCREEN

Città Castellana : Duomo. Drudus and Lucas Cosmatus

48. TOMB OF CARDINAL GUGLIELMO FIESCHI

Rome: S. Lorenzo fuori le Mura

49. TOMB OF LUCA SAVELLI AND FAMILY

Rome: S. Maria in Aracoeli

50. DETAIL OF TOMB OF POPE CLEMENT IV

Viterbo: S. Francesco. Petrus Oderisi

51. TOMB OF POPE CLEMENT IV

Viterbo: S. Francesco. Petrus Oderisi

53. TOMB OF CARDINAL CONSALVO RODRIGUEZ

Rome: S. Maria Maggiore. Johannes Cosmatus

54. PAVEMENT

Rome: S. Maria in Cosmedin

55.   DETAIL OF PAVEMENT

Rome: S. Clemente

56. DETAIL OF PAVEMENT

Rome: S. Giovanni in Laterano

57. DETAIL OF PAVEMENT

Rome: S. Giovanni in Laterano

58. PANEL OF PAVEMENT

Rome: S. Maria Maggiore

59. DETAIL OF PAVEMENT

Rome: S. Maria in Aracoeli

60. DETAIL OF PAVEMENT

Anagni: Duomo Crypt (S. Magnus). Cosmas and his sons Lucas and Jacobus (1231)

61. DETAIL OF PAVEMENT

Farfa Sabina : Badia. Rainaldus

62. DETAIL OF PAVEMENT

Farfa Sabina: Badia. Rainaldus

63. SANCTUARY PAVEMENT

London: Westminster Abbey. Odericus. (? Petrus Oderisi)

After an Aquatint in Ackermann's 'Westminster Abbey' (1812)

64. PAVEMENT

Canterbury: Cathedral. S. Thomas's Chapel. (? Petrus Oderisi)